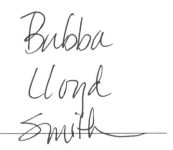

LITERATURE AND BELIEF

Edited by Alan L. Berger
and Jesse S. Crisler

Literature and Belief
Volume 26.1

Center for the Study of Christian Values in Literature

BRIGHAM YOUNG UNIVERSITY

LITERATURE AND BELIEF
A biannual publication of the Center for the Study
of Christian Values in Literature
College of Humanities
Brigham Young University

Jesse S. Crisler, Director   Daniel K. Muhlestein, Associate Director

EDITORS
Jesse S. Crisler, Editor
Daniel K. Muhlestein, Associate Editor
Melvin J. Thorne, Managing Editor
Jane D. Brady, Production Editor
Lance E. Larsen, Poetry Editor

EDITORIAL BOARD
Thayle Anderson, Murray State University
Marilyn Arnold, Brigham Young University (emeritus)
Alan Berger, Florida Atlantic University
John F. Desmond, Whitman College
James Dougherty, University of Notre Dame
Bruce L. Edwards, Bowling Green State University
J. Karl Franson, University of Maine at Farmington
Thomas E. (Ted) Lyon, Brigham Young University
Dorothy Huff Oberhaus, Mercy College

The opinions expressed by contributors to LITERATURE AND BELIEF are their own and do not necessarily reflect the views of The Church of Jesus Christ of Latter-day Saints, Brigham Young University, or the editors. LITERATURE AND BELIEF considers scholarly, interpretive articles that focus on moral/religious literary issues, book reviews, interviews, and also poetry. Manuscripts should conform to *The MLA Style Manual*. LITERATURE AND BELIEF is indexed in the *MLA International Bibliography*, *Abstracts of English Studies*, *American Humanities Index* (*AHI*), and *Literary Criticism Register*. This journal is a member of CELJ, the Council of Learned Journals.

Subscription cost is $10.00; $14.00 outside the USA.
Address all correspondence, submission, and subscription inquiries to
Literature and Belief, 3184 JFSB, Brigham Young University, Provo, UT 84602
(801) 422-3073

Vol. 26.1   2006

Back Cover: View of Jewish cemetery, Sighet, Romania

Contents

BOOK REVIEWS

POETRY

EDITOR'S PREFACE

Elie Wiesel, Holocaust survivor and Nobel Peace laureate, has for over a half-century born eloquent witness on behalf of the victims of the Jewish tragedy. That witness is inextricably bound to memory, a theme, he attests, that "dominates all my obsessions . . . because I fear forgetfulness as much as hatred and death" (*From* 9). But his is a witness that carries the burden of the struggle between the necessity to speak and the impossibility of finding adequate words. Speech vies constantly with silence in his work; or, rather, he seeks to give voice to silence. He brings his readers near the "fiery gates" of the *Shoah* but knows that only survivors can possibly fathom what occurred in the Kingdom of Night. And yet, to use the author's favorite phrase, his message is one of hope against despair.

Profoundly rooted in Judaism—its classical sources and its legends—Wiesel's message has great universal resonance. Furthermore, his words are addressed as well to generations born after the Holocaust. He has influenced people all over the world: Jews, Christians, Muslims, Hindus, Buddhists, believers and skeptics alike. It is no accident that his Nobel citation calls him a "messenger to mankind" (Aarvik 4). He has, in the tradition of a great teacher, "raised up many disciples." As writer, lecturer, and teacher, Wiesel ceaselessly works on behalf of human rights. He has written more than forty books in French, and his works have been translated into English, Dutch, German, Japanese, and Norwegian. Included in his literary prizes are the Prix Médicis for *A Beggar in Jerusalem* (1970) and the Prix Rivarel for *The Town Beyond the Wall* (1964). Furthermore, he is a recipient of the Presidential Medal of Freedom, the United States Congressional Gold Medal, the Medal of Liberty, the Ellis Island Medal of Honor, and the French Legion of Honor with the rank of Grand Cross. Wiesel is Andrew W. Mellon Professor in the Humanities and University Professor at Boston University.

For Wiesel literature and theology intersect. In his interview with me, he attests that he wishes his prayers to be turned into stories. These post-Holocaust prayers are addressed both to God and to humanity. His novels, poems, cantatas, and plays consistently raise and re-raise the central post-Holocaust questions: where was God; where was humanity; why were there so few helpers in the Kingdom of Night? Furthermore, Wiesel is more interested in questions than in answers. "In the word question," notes Wiesel, "there is a beautiful word—quest. I love that word. We are all partners in a quest"

("Wrestling"). Questions keep open the possibility of dialogue. It is answers which divide humanity. The Final Solution to the Jewish "Problem" was an answer. It brought death to six million Jews and destruction to the European continent and wrought havoc on all pre-Holocaust civilizational and theological assumptions.

Although Wiesel refers to himself as a storyteller, his tales are fraught with theological significance. Cardinal Jean-Marie Lustiger terms him "*one of the great theologians* of [the twentieth] century" (188). Lustiger defines a theologian in terms that underscore Wiesel's distinctive voice: "whoever questions and even challenges God, all the while desiring to obey His Word and listening to His silence, that person *is* a theologian" (189). Wiesel's questioning and challenging of God and of humanity mark him as one of the most important writers of our time. A brand plucked from the fire, he seeks to effect a *tikkun olam* (mending or repair of the world) in order that his past does not become humanity's future. He views writing as an act of correcting injustice.

Contributors to this issue, Jews and Christians, shed light on several of the myriad themes that emerge from Wiesel's vast *oeuvre*. He is a teacher as well as a writer. He views the two roles as being intimately related, observing that "the writer in me is a teacher, the teacher in me is a writer" (*And* 111). Martha Liptzin Hauptman's reflection, the Afterword of this issue, emphasizes Wiesel's role as teacher and mentor. She notes the "stunning metamorphosis of young people [at Boston University] exposed to a master teacher, eminent humanitarian, and humane soul who deeply believes in them and in their impact on the future." Two essays focus on the relationship between literature and theology in Wiesel's work. David Patterson stresses the importance of recognizing him as a *Jewish* writer whose tales are framed by Aggadah, for Wiesel's tales subtly yet consistently "link literature and revelation." Thomas A. Idinopulos discusses the meaning for Christians of Wiesel's classic memoir *Night* (1960). He contends that its scene of the boy on the gallows is a reminder that Christ's sacrifice was in vain: it produced "not new human life but more Jewish blood."

Victoria Aarons and Ellen Fine discuss Wiesel's work from a literary-psychological angle. Aarons analyzes *The Gates of the Forest* (1966) in terms of its "strategy of condensation," which she identifies as a key element in the novel. Wiesel's portrayal of a Passion play is a "play within a play," transforming "time, place, and identity as it reenacts past trauma." Fine's study analyzes Wiesel as a "second degree witness" (*un témoignage modeste, au second degré*), one who witnesses his own witness. Consequently, his two-volume memoirs are "both a continuation of his fiction and a commentary on it": his life is a commentary on his texts.

Suzanne Lundquist and Hannah Berliner Fischthal address different issues raised by Wiesel in his memoirs, *All Rivers Run to the Sea: Memoirs* (1995) and *And the Sea Is Never Full: Memoirs, 1969–* (1999). Lundquist, who terms these works "autoethnographies," ponders the "unacknowledged power of the feminine" and the role it plays in Wiesel's "capacity to survive in the face of abhorrent memories." Berliner Fischthal pursues the intriguing question of why Wiesel, a devoted Hasid, refers to I. L. Peretz, a socialist "who satirized rebbes and their disciples," as his "hero." She finds that both writers "seek justice and espouse means to elevate the poor," while "punctuat[ing] their tales with doubts and questions."

In his interview with me, Wiesel addresses the significance of the appearance of a fiftieth-anniversary edition of *Night* in a new translation by his wife Marion; comments on his novel *The Time of the Uprooted* (2005), in which female characters play a central role; speaks of Jewish/Christian relations, which he views as never having been better; notes with alarm the rise of fanaticism in religion; addresses the threat posed by radical Islamicists who, by killing in the name of God, turn their deity into a killer; and emphasizes the post-Auschwitz moral role of the writer.

I thank Bonnie Lander for her skill and patience in important clerical tasks; the contributors to this issue for their valuable essays; Sergei Bermeniev for permission to reproduce his photograph of Wiesel on the cover of this issue; Rachel Straus, Wiesel's personal assistant, for providing photographs of Wiesel's office and Wiesel himself; Gloria Cronin, Department of English, Brigham Young University; and Jesse S. Crisler, editor of *Literature and Belief*, for helping to make this special issue a reality. Most of all, I am indebted to the voice, vision, and person of Elie Wiesel for his friendship and inspiration. In a world darkened by hatred, violence, and indifference, Wiesel's moral voice is a beacon of hope. Like the Just person about whom he writes, his efforts on behalf of humanity continue, even if at times no one seems to be listening. He continues to shout in order to prevent the world from changing him.

–Alan L. Berger
Guest Editor

Works Cited

Aarvik, Egil. "The Nobel Presentation Speech." *Elie Wiesel: The Nobel Peace Prize 1986*. New York: Summit Books, 1986. 3–11.

Lustiger, Jean-Marie. "*Night*: The Absence of God? The Presence of God? A Meditation in Three Parts." *Elie Wiesel: Between Memory and Hope*. Ed. Carol Rittner. New York: New York UP, 1990. 188–96.

Wiesel, Elie. *And the Sea is Never Full: Memoirs, 1969–*. Trans. Marion Wiesel. New York: Alfred A. Knopf, 1999.

———. *From the Kingdom of Memory: Reminiscences*. New York: Schocken Books, 1995.

———. "Wrestling with God and Questions of Forgiveness." Tanner Lecture on Human Values, Snow College, Ephraim, UT. 22 May 2006.

Arioso on Wings

*I am still confident of this: I will see the goodness of the Lord in the land
of the living.* Psalm 27:13

A trumpet trills like the throat of a lily,
Vibrato on a bumblebee's tongue,
While *Arioso for Brass* plays and I watch
Sheep grazing on the knoll,
Moving clumsily along every few minutes
Like leaves in a lazy breeze,
Bumping into one another, head
To wool-wadded rump. Blackbirds dart
In and out of the cherry trees, drinking in the ruby
Juice like Bach's melody imbibes smooth
Intonations. Beneath morning sun,
Last night's rainwater sluices
Through the creek bed, a swelling epiphany
Spilling over the hillside. Nearby, the neighbor's dog
Digs a hole, plunging his nose
Into his earthen bowl. In the pasture, geese
Splash in puddles as the cows
Dip their necks and in perfect harmony,
Tug at the wet blades like notes on a soul.
One cranes her neck toward her flank, shoots
Out her tongue to lick at a fly-
Induced itch, her black fur rippling,
Tail twirling. Another lows like a tuba.
And it is goodness, isn't it?, here in the land
Of the living, riding on this silken air,
Sliding like a trombone through the whorls
Of corn, pulsing like green,
Iridescent on the hummingbird's wings.

–Julie L. Moore

A NEW TRANSLATION BY MARION WIESEL

Night

WITH A NEW PREFACE BY THE AUTHOR

ELIE WIESEL

WINNER OF THE NOBEL PEACE PRIZE

"A slim volume of terrifying power."
—*The New York Times*

Book
OPRAH'S
Club

Cover of Marion Wiesel's new translation of *Night*, marking the
novel's fiftieth anniversary

Interview with Elie Wiesel,
February 23, 2006

Alan L. Berger
Florida Atlantic University

ALB: Our conversation is being held against the backdrop of a world in turmoil, an increase in state-sponsored anti-Semitism, an existential threat made to Israel, terrorism in the name of God, genocide in Darfur, among other places. What are your thoughts at this moment in history?

EW: I am feeling rather melancholy because I have, together with so many millions and millions of people, hoped that the twenty-first century would be a better and surely not a worse one. There was so much hope and so much fervor and so much enthusiasm. It was burning in us and you felt it throughout the planet. Here we are in the sixth year of the century and hatred is ravaging the human heart, there are more and more conflicts, fanaticism is reigning over hundreds of millions of people, and the open threats to each other and, especially, to Israel, the oldest scapegoat. Anyone who needs a target turns against us and, as you mentioned, for the very first time a head of state came out and said that he wants Israel to be wiped off the surface of the earth. The madness of his statement! Does he think of what it would do to the Jewish people and what it would do regarding humanity as such? So, I am skeptical of my own work. I feel, when I say I, I mean the witness in me was convinced that the world would be a better world because of those of us who bear witness. We try to bear witness. Surely the last year many of us have tried to warn people, the world, to say, "look: whatever happened to the Jewish people is only the beginning." And the witness's testimony was not received. Otherwise, the world would be a safer world.

ALB: Our discussion also coincides with the appearance of the fiftieth-anniversary edition of *Night* and the publication of your recent novel *The Time of the Uprooted* (2005). Can you comment on the connection that you see?

EW: What I say in my preface is true: had it not been for *Night*, I would not have written anything else. If there had been no war, I would have stayed in my *shtetl*, my small village, and become a local *Rosh Yeshivah*. That was my goal. And here I am. Together with you, we teach and we write and try to communicate. Certain experiences cannot be communicated, but still we try. As you know—you know my work better than many others, Alan—it is a mosaic. One brings the other, one is linked to the other. And if you remove one from this body of work, the whole edifice can collapse. But the fundament, the foundation, is *Night*. In *The Uprooted*, I felt a whole century was uprooted, as was history itself. I felt the divinity of God was uprooted, which is a mystical concept. We call it the *galut* of the *Shekhinah*: the exile of the *Shekhinah*. Therefore, I wrote it like that. But then I just finished another novel, because it takes me four or five years to write a novel.

ALB: And what is it called?

EW: In French it is called *Un désir fou de danser* (2006), *A Mad Desire to Dance*. It is about madness. I always have a madman in every one of my books. In my other books he is usually a secondary character. In this one he is the principle protagonist. It came out in

France in May. I have always been obsessed with the notion that history *can* go mad. Just as history could be uprooted and everything else with it. The Time of the Uprooted is the twentieth century.

ALB: Indeed it is.

EW: And as for *Night* the difference is that my wife re-translated it. It is amazing what one woman could have done. I mean Oprah. The book appeared in 1955, '56 in Yiddish, nearly fifty years ago in Argentina. In two or three weeks, the new version sold more than a million copies and all of a sudden was on the bestseller list. Oprah has extraordinary power, extraordinary moral power.

ALB: You once wrote in *One Generation After* (1970) that one of the Just Men, a *Lamed Vav Zaddik*, comes to Sodom to save its inhabitants, and despite his preaching nothing changed and a child, moved by compassion, asks the preacher why he continued since his words have no visible effect. And the Just Man replied, "In the beginning, I thought I could change man. Today, I know I cannot. If I shout today, if I still scream, it is," he attests, "to prevent man from ultimately changing me" (72).

EW: I am the same person who wrote that story then, and I would write it again now the same way. I would not change a word. The tale is still valid. I remain the same. I consider myself the same Hasid of my town, a *Yeshiva Bucher*. I did not change much. If the experience *then* did not change me, does anybody think that a Nobel Prize can change me?

ALB: But the world has yet to learn completely.

EW: Of course. My worry is that *they* try everything. They try sometimes to change you by seduction. In one of my novels, *The Oath* (1973), a preacher comes and speaks. Instead of screaming and shouting at him they applaud him. It is the worst compliment they can give him.

ALB: I want to pursue this issue. What is the role of the witness in these turbulent and terror-filled times? I am thinking of Moshe the Beadle: is he the paradigm of the plight of the witness destined to be unheard?

EW: To me he was the first and therefore he was the most tragic of all. He tried to tell the tale. He tried to tell the tale and I remember it because he told it to me. Nobody wanted to listen, and I myself did not believe him. As I say in my memoir, people did not believe him. And I love stories. And I felt sorry for him. I did listen. But I did not believe. And then I saw him, he was part of the first transport. In retrospect, I remember his face, he started shaking his head as if to say, "I warned you. I warned you."

ALB: And you wrote about that in *Night*.

EW: In retrospect, if someone else had warned us . . . had Churchill, Stalin, or Roosevelt sent a message on the radio, at that time we listened to the B.B.C., "Jews of Hungary, do not go. Do not board the trains," many of us would have gone into hiding. There were people who were Christians. . . . Our maid pleaded with us. She implored us with tears in her eyes to accompany her to the mountains where she had a hut but again we did not know. Nobody warned us. But later on I remember Moshe the Beadle. So he, of course, is to me the first witness. But since then, I believe that his tragedy was that he was not believed. When a witness comes and speaks and nobody listens . . . woe to him.

ALB: You wrote about *Night* that it was the end of everything and the beginning of everything, and I want to ask about then and now. What has changed and what remains the same? One thing that is changed is the recognition of the Holocaust by the culture at large. Education, of course, has improved. So it seems that at least part of the witness's testimony is being heard.

EW: It is. And it is not. Take Darfur today. Our protests worked. It did not help the people there but at least there is a lot about their suffering in the media. I was one of the first to sound the alarm on Darfur. Did it help much? I am not sure, but Colin Powell and Kofi Annan went there. United Nations observers are there. More military will come. In Rwanda, nobody cared. Nobody. 600,000 or 800,000 people could have been saved and were not.

ALB: Why do you think that is?

EW: Maybe because it was the end of the century. People were tired or became numb.

ALB: Which is a danger.

EW: Which is a danger. When it comes to our own subject that you and I are so involved in, reminding the people of what happened in the past, the danger is numbness.

ALB: Can this pitfall be avoided?

EW: That is why I stopped. I could not teach this subject. I admire you for doing it. I cannot. I taught it for two years and it was difficult. Very difficult. Therefore, I was spared the danger of numbness. But I can imagine the high school teacher who teaches this course every single day. That teacher must at one point become numb. One cannot repeat the same poem and cry, one simply cannot. Maybe some do, I do not know how. Therefore there *is* a danger there. And if I protested the T.V. docudrama *Holocaust*, it is for that reason: because it appeals to what is cheap in people. I would like our destiny to appeal to what is purest and most noble, generous, and compassionate in a human being, not what is kitsch.

ALB: Some things remained the same since *Night*: anti-Semitism, prejudice, contempt for the other. Concerning anti-Semitism, you once observed that at Auschwitz its victims died, but the disease remained. Do you see an end to this bi-millennial pathology which is the crutch on which tyrants perpetually lean?

EW: Alan, I said in the same context, "if Auschwitz didn't cure the world of anti-Semitism, what will?" But there will always be anti-Semites. At the least we should protest against those anti-Semites and surely against the system that condones anti-Semitism. In France there was a young Jew, Ilan Halimi, who was kidnapped. He was caught by a band of twenty so-called "Barbarians." They were convinced that because he was a Jew they would get money; stereotypically all Jews are rich. They tortured him and they killed him. In the beginning the police simply said it was a matter of ransom. Then they realized that it was an anti-Semitic act. In France they have laws against anti-Semitism. So, things are changing in some places.

ALB: I think that the French president went to his funeral. Is that true?

EW: It is possible. I would not be surprised.

ALB: It is a terrible scandal and a personal tragedy.

EW: Every murder is a tragedy. Last year French Jews were worried. The wave of anti-Semitism hit France. Jews were afraid to wear a kipa on the street.

ALB: Do you foresee in the near future a massive aliyah of French Jews?

EW: This I do not know. But all over Europe, wherever I would go, people would come to me asking something that should worry me even more. They did not say, should we leave? They asked, *when* should we leave? That is more traumatic.

ALB: That is very frightening.

EW: But then, the French government, I must say, did everything it could to take measures, extraordinary measures, against anti-Semitism and the anti-Semites. That quieted down the situation.

ALB: So the measures had some effect?

EW: Yes, they had an effect.

ALB: You write in the introduction to the new edition of *Night* that the *Shoah* was a war against Jewish memory. Yet again we are hearing the ominous rantings of deniers. I know it is a complex question, but what is it about the Jewish historical presence that our enemies wish to extirpate?

EW: They cannot leave the Jews alone. These people cannot let the Jews live in peace. I say the world is a world for all of us. God created the world; He was not the God of the Jews. God in *Bereyshit* is God of all people, not only of the children of Israel.

ALB: That message is frequently ignored.

EW: But they also say we cannot live *with* you. This means you do not deserve to live and therefore we do whatever we can to deprive you of the taste for living, of the passion for living and of life itself. Sometimes I am asked at international conferences, why are you Jews hated so much? And I say, why do you ask *me*? Why should I make the hater's task easier? Ask the hater.

ALB: I want to return briefly to the Oprah show. Your decision to appear, like many things associated with the *Shoah*, brought some controversy in its wake. I assume that you view it as a teaching moment, an occasion to educate a new generation.

EW: I did not ask to appear. I did not realize that the controversy about James Frey had implicated, though lightly, *Night*. Some articles said that she wanted to atone for defending Frey.

ALB: I read that.

EW: That was the controversy. But was there a controversy about my appearing on it? I did not see it.

ALB: Let me suggest one.

EW: Please.

ALB: There are many junior scholars hoping to gain a reputation by attacking the giants. They are looking for discrepancies in the two translations.

EW: I am the one who said it in my memoir, *All Rivers Run to the Sea* (1995).

ALB: You brought it out. I know.

EW: I put it in the memoir myself, of course. That is why I did not wait for them to say so.

ALB: Your readers understand this.

EW: I quoted and wrote full passages which came out in 1994.

ALB: The careful reader is aware of this fact.

EW: It came out in 1994 in France and here in '95. But I am the one who revealed it. We must be honest about these kinds of things.

ALB: Precisely.

EW: You said that there was controversy about my appearance on "Oprah," but I have not heard anything.

ALB: For example, some might emphasize a disparity which appears on a certain page in the two editions. But, more importantly, are you concerned that the necessary dialectic between speech and silence and the insufficiency of language itself which you emphasize in the introduction to *Night* are nuances which will be lost in popular culture?

EW: It is quite possible, but who knows? Look, I have to be I. Come back to the story of the Just Man. I cannot let others govern my life. Or my writing, or my attitude toward writing, or what I think. I am not the sole possessor of truth. I write and write and yet I am drawn to silence. That is what I do, I cut and cut.

ALB: And it is very effective. Have you taken Oprah to Auschwitz yet?

EW:.   Yes.

ALB: What was that experience like?

EW: She is a great lady. Some ten or twelve years ago she already had a program on *Night* and interviewed me.

ALB: I read about that. It is a remarkable story.

EW: It was Oprah's idea to go with me to Auschwitz. She actually came to Auschwitz on her birthday. She gave up her birthday in Chicago and we went there. She has tremendous sensitivity. I will give you an example. I came from a conference. She was there already. And she told her people that she does not want to see me before. The first meeting must be in Auschwitz. She did not want to have small talk. That is the truth. And the way she behaved there, in that place, was admirable.

ALB: You may not feel comfortable commenting on this, but do you think she had done much reading in preparation?

EW: She had to. When she interviewed me the first time, she knew *Night* by heart. And again now, she has read a lot, she knows a lot, she wants to learn more. I have great admiration for her.

ALB: I want to switch to *The Time of the Uprooted*, which I find a richly complex novel that raises many philosophical and religious issues. It also appears to be a departure from your earlier writings in that the female characters are more fully drawn and at least two of them, Ilonka and Dr. Lilly Rosenkrantz, play salvific roles. Would you comment on this?

EW: I have been criticized in the past that all of my main heroes are men. In every novel of mine the feminine presence is there, but this time more than before. Life is mixture. Art seeks to discern what makes the two one. And literature is a refined word for the metamorphosis of that artistic endeavor. The women here of course are actually great. Even Gamaliel's unhappy wife. His wife wishes to help him. What did she want? To make him happy. And because he *could not* be happy, she could not understand him.

ALB: And she was unable to succeed.

EW: So it was her failure *and* his failure, it was a double failure. The book is a despairing book. But the story is not an appeal of despair. It is a desperate appeal for hope. Everyone wants hope. But it is also up-rooted. The writer who writes for other people, under their names. And finally, when he writes his own book, he does not finish it.

ALB: Why not?

EW: Because the Messiah has not come. So how does he finish it? By personal redemption. Everyone has a tragedy there and the only way for this tragic character to find any redemption is through others. So at the end, of course, it is more hopeful. It remains a question mark: who was that woman?

ALB: We do not know her identity.

EW: We do not know. Except I hint: is that the two Shabbat candles? Maybe it is another woman, but who knows, maybe not.

ALB: It could refer to the universality of the Jewish experience.

EW: Of the Jewish experience, exactly.

ALB: Gamaliel's identity is clearly an issue. Forced to change his name because of the *Shoah*, he becomes Péter, he has to learn Christian rituals, he must hide his whereabouts and remain silent. He clearly emblemizes the plight of the refugee and all those who, as you say, have been uprooted in that terrible century. Do you think he represents the state of post-Auschwitz humanity?

EW: Absolutely. I believe that whatever happened to humanity in general happened to Jews first. It is not a statement of superiority. It is simply the universality of our experience. Never before has an entire people been not only uprooted but out-rooted the way we were during the Second World War. Since then it happened to others. It is not the same event though. I never compare. But these things happen to others. Supposedly uprooted is a condition that is a twentieth-century product. Never before have so many people been uprooted, become refugees, immigrants, and illegals. No one here in America is illegal, they are uprooted. So therefore Gamaliel represents all of them, and therefore he and his three friends, what did they do? They became a self-appointed United Nations to try to help those immigrants with papers or with social help or even to find a husband for the poor woman who needs a husband for her daughter.

ALB: They were the shining example of humanity.

EW: Absolutely they were, yes.

ALB: For me, this novel raises a disturbing question about the future of Holocaust memory. Gamaliel has two estranged daughters. But unlike *The Forgotten* (1992) in which you portray a loving relationship between Elhanan and Malkiel, both of whom are committed to embrace memory, although on different levels, *The Time of the Uprooted* suggests that Gamaliel's memory or a portion at least would be committed to paper in *The Book of Secrets*, but what about the second generation?

EW: We do not know. We do not know. They may come back. But for the moment we are seeing among the young people an attraction to India mainly. To Nepal. To the Orient in general. To leave western culture behind.

ALB: Among Israelis as well.

EW: It is almost a rule in Israel that soldiers at the end of their military service go to India or Tibet. I try to understand why. Why Tibet? And the only answer I could find is that the Orient had nothing to do with the Holocaust. All the other countries had somehow a relationship to it, except the Orient. Therefore, they want to go away. The Dalai Lama, my friend, is a great hero to them. It is because Tibetan monks have nothing to do with the Holocaust.

ALB: But yet you write in your autobiography that you went to India.

EW: But I left it. I studied the *Vedas*. *The Upanishads*. Extraordinary texts. But they weren't for me.

ALB: Why weren't they for you?

EW: I am a Jew. It is through Jewishness that I find universality, not through denying it.

ALB: Gamaliel loves stories, and I am reminded of your father's unfinished story in *Night*, but Gamaliel's literary efforts are on two levels. He is a ghostwriter for a "famous novelist." But his own authentic meditations are contained in *The Book of Secrets*. What are the secrets? Is he also the ghost of either himself or those murdered in the *Shoah*?

EW: He is not that ambitious. Not that pretentious. But he seemed to believe he must find the words. That is what I felt all my life. The need to find the words. I am not sure I found them but I try. That is why for others it is easy to write, or in another's name, whatever they want, but for oneself, in one's name it is different. But to come back to what you say about the two daughters, it is the most tragic chapter in the novel. The two daughters denied their father. And therefore, Gamaliel may have another child with Rosenkrantz.

ALB: She is also a healer.

EW: I hint that hope is not to be excluded.

*   *   *   *   *   *   *   *   *

ALB: I wonder if we could switch for a moment to the issue of Jewish-Christian relations. In a *Beggar in Jerusalem* (1970), you have Shlomo reporting on an imagined meeting with Yeoshua: "you think you are suffering for my sake and for my brothers, yet we are the ones who have been made to suffer for you because of you" (56). After hearing what the future held in store for the Jewish people, Jesus attests that he wants his heritage to be a gift of compassion and hope, not punishment in blood, but it was already too late. How do you see contemporary interfaith dialogue?

EW: I am much more optimistic now than before. It has to do with Pope John XXIII. He was the great man in Christianity. He was the first to open the church, to admit its failings, and to correct the liturgy omitting all the insulting sentences. And then he was followed by John Paul II.

ALB: Pope Paul VI and then John Paul the II.

EW: Paul VI was not our friend.

ALB: No indeed. John XXIII intervened, as you know, to have the word deicide removed from *Nostra Aetate* (1965).

EW: But the next pope, John Paul II, was good. Though not in the beginning. I had big problems with him in the beginning. Why?

Because the first thing he did was go to Auschwitz, which I liked. He managed to be there and deliver many homilies, but he did not once mention the word Jew there. Never. He went only to see the graves of Edith Stein, a Jewish woman who became a Carmelite, and Maximilian Kolbe, an anti-Semitic Polish priest who did a heroic thing when he chose to die in place of a cellmate. But I must say that afterwards John Paul II improved a lot. He changed. He was the first pope to go to a synagogue. He was the first pope to visit Israel, Jerusalem, the Kotel, and Yad Vashem; and he had a musical commemoration of the *Shoah* in the Vatican. But, never have Jewish-Christian relations been as good as they are now.

ALB: Yet the Vatican continues to send mixed signals concerning the Holocaust. The beatification of Edith Stein that you mentioned and the, I think, completely inexplicable beatification of Pius IX.

EW: There are so many groups there and so many currents, trends, influences, policies, bureaucracies, and theologies, it is not one monolithic institution.

ALB: Jules Isaac when he went to see John XXIII, as you know, requested that "a voice from the summit" speak.

EW: But John XXIII did. Jules Isaac knew him from before, that is why he sought him. They spent three days and three nights together. "May I leave you with hope," he asked. And the Pope said, "You deserve more than that."

ALB: Anecdotally, there is a story about John XXIII being asked how many people work in the Vatican, and his response was, "about half."

EW: And the question should be, which half? Now the new Pope, let us wait and see. For the moment I think he is following in the footsteps of John XXIII.

ALB: Several of your works refer to the *Hasidei Umot haOlam* (Right-eous Gentiles), beginning with *Night* and the police inspector who per-haps tried to warn your father, *The Gates of the Forest* (1966) certainly, *The Trial of God* (1979), and your autobiography. Two questions: What do you think motivated the moral minority, and why so few?

EW: These are the questions I ask them. When I was chairman of the United States Holocaust Memorial Council, I organized a confer-ence called The Courage to Care.

ALB: I remember attending that conference.

EW: I brought people together. Those who saved and those whom they saved. I would go from one of the rescuers to the other asking, what made you heroic? And they said, Oh come on, we are not he-roes. Do not call us heroes. One of them said, when you see a child running in the street from pursuers, do you not open the door? If your neighbor is hungry will you deny him a slice of bread? I remem-ber George Schultz, the Secretary of State, was at the opening cere-mony. He was a very close friend. That is when I said in those times, "Woe to us, it was enough to be human to become a hero" ("Against"). There is one story which I heard, a beautiful story. A woman in Berlin was honored as a Righteous Gentile because she saved a family. A simple woman, just like our maid. And the jour-nalists asked, "why did you do it, why did you do it?" She pulled herself up and said, "I will tell you why: out of self-respect."

ALB: *Kol Hakavod.*

EW: Therefore, I do not know why they think there was no choice. When you hear about the onlookers, the bystanders, who said, we could not do a thing, I say, nonsense. There *was* a choice. Always.

ALB: To go to the other end of that continuum, what do you think the uproar over the Mel Gibson movie, *The Passion of the Christ*, tells us about Jewish-Christian dialogue?

EW: I call it the Second Crucifixion of Jesus. I did not want to enter the polemic then. It is not for me; it is undignified. I saw the film, I thought it was a bad film. But it *was* anti-Semitic. And why? He showed his hand at the end. All of a sudden you noticed far away the Jewish Temple burning, and whom do you see then? The devil among the Jews. What does it mean? The Temple was burning because we Jews did not recognize Christ. Because we crucified Christ. This is exactly what Christian anti-Semitism has been re-peating for centuries and centuries. The film is anti-Semitic—but I did not want to enter the debate.

ALB: Many, many others did, and I think that what it showed was that despite how much distance we have come, we still have a ways to go.

EW: Right.

ALB: Elsewhere, you have commented about the difference be-tween the Crusades and Auschwitz.

EW: I felt for a long time and I still do that Christianity, because of what has been done to the Jews, lost many of its values in Auschwitz. In a way it was a defeat of Christianity, because it happened in the heart of Europe which was a Christian continent. Both Catholics and Protestants were baptized. Hitler himself was baptized. But to compare it to the Crusades, no. The Crusades were in a way actually worse be-cause they did whatever they did in the name of Christ. The crusaders carried a crucifix. They went and killed and killed in the name of Christ. In Germany they did *not* kill in the name of Christ. They did it for Germany, for German power, for German glory, for German in-terests. What they said was for the sake of Germany and not for Jesus. To make things easier for the Catholics? No I do not think so. They have enough to atone for and Christians have enough to reflect on. And by the way, the fact that the Christians were killers, that hurts the good young Germans. They do not sleep at night. The killers were Christians. But only the killers are guilty.

ALB: Do you see a certain irony in the fact that when the Christians were going on the Crusades they viewed the Jews and the Muslims as infidels? Now, the Muslims view the Christians and the Jews as infidels.

EW: For Jews nothing changed. Nothing changed because this hatred of the Jews is so deeply rooted in so many nations' memories. For some reason they need it. Why should the president of Iran need that? His problem is not with Israel, there are no common borders between Iran and Israel. His problem is not with Jerusalem under Jewish control. But he feels he cannot live otherwise except when he preaches hatred toward the Jewish people.

ALB: One wonders about the Jewish community in Iran and what will happen to them.

EW: There are 25,000 Iranian Jews.

ALB: 25,000 hostages.

EW: They are. When the Shah left so many left and went to Israel and to America. I am worried, but I am a worrier.

ALB: But you are also a doer.

EW: I try, I try, but I am a worrier.

ALB: How do you interpret the response in much of the Muslim world to the cartoons depicting Mohammed that were published in a Danish newspaper?

EW: Obviously, a cartoon is disrespectful to Mohammed. What was the disrespect? In Islam the image of Mohammed should not be shown. We Jews do not have that attitude. For us only God's image should not be shown. There were so many images of Moses made afterwards. Michelangelo made a sculpture. Did we protest? Did we organize demonstrations in the street against it? But the Muslims have a right to their belief and we should respect each other's beliefs. I believe in such respect. As you know, we are duty bound to respect the others and the Jew in me has respect for Christians who are really believing Christians, who respect others. I have the same respect for Muslims who are Muslims and respect others for what they are. Therefore those who printed the cartoon should acknowledge their disrespect. But from there to organize world-wide demonstrations with violence and with burnings is too much. And the attacking of embassies, beating up people, that is outrageous. It is out of order. Is *that* their religion? Is this what Mohammed taught them? Is *that* what the Koran teaches them? At the same time I am worried about who is organizing this. This is like a wildfire lit by the fanatics. Does it mean that Islam is now seeking to conquer what it lost? With what they are trying to do to Israel, who knows? I do not know. I am worried about the reaction. As distasteful as the cartoon was, the reaction to it was equally out of place. It was uncivilized; it was a protest against civilization, against the other, against humanity, against their own beliefs. I hope that some of them know that. A religion which preaches only violence must become a victim of that violence and I hope it is not so. There are a few journalists there who write articles urging Islam to stop the bloodshed. Good for them. I would give these journalists prizes for they need courage to say that or do that but they are so few, so terribly few.

ALB: What do you say about the double standard here? Certain Arab newspapers print very offensive images of Jesus and publish the noxious forgery, *Protocols of the Elders of Zion.*

EW: What they show on television, my God, what they show on television: Rabbis drinking blood and killing children for Passover to bake matzoh. Where do we live now? If we Jews had used the same method, can you imagine what would have been after the Holocaust? We would have turned the whole world into a flame.

ALB: You mean we would have incinerated the world?

EW: Absolutely. What we *could* have done but we did not. We don't believe in that kind of response. We believe in trying to find an answer. The only answer must be a humanizing one.

ALB: You wrote in *Somewhere A Master* (1982) that the Besht was the first to publicly proclaim that "the way to God leads through your fellow man" (151). This Islamic fury is in fact killing in the name of God.

EW: They do not realize that when they do that, they turn their God into a killer. That is a fanatic, that is what we see in history. The fanatic is making God at least an accomplice when he invokes God's name. He turns his God into a killer.

ALB: How can we Christians and Jews reach out to Islam, when the tradition does not appear to have undergone a period of self-critical theological reflection?

EW: Education, only by education. Do not use violence to stop violence. Whatever the answer, and I must have said it elsewhere, education must be its major component.

ALB: Are there voices on the other side willing to listen?

EW: Not for the moment. Most of them are afraid, but I am not giving up hope.

*   *   *   *   *   *   *   *   *

ALB: What is the role of the writer today? You share Rebbe Nahman of Bratzlav's aspiration that your tales should be understood as prayers. You wrote in *Paroles d'étranger* (1982) that "hopefully no one will be able to distinguish between the ones, stories, and the others, prayers. Not even myself. And, myself less than anyone else" (180, Berger's translation).

EW: Yes. But I wrote about prayer a lot in *The Town Beyond the Wall* (1964) which is one of my earliest novels. It is divided not into four chapters but four prayers. I think our capacity for prayer, our need for prayer, our ability to pray, and our hope, there is hope in prayer, mean the prayers will be received. As always, since my child-hood, we would pray and, therefore, like Rebbe Nahman of Bratzlav, of whom I am a great admirer as you know, who would like his sto-ries to be turned into prayers. I would like *my* prayers to be told, to be turned into stories. The question is, why should God need our prayer? Why should God need our flattery? How come He is not re-ally repulsed by all that? And there is only one answer I have. God does not need our prayers. We need them. We need to be able to pray in sincerity and beauty. And the prayer should not be against somebody but always for somebody. That is a true prayer, when it is for someone else, not for yourself.

ALB: Who is listening to these prayers and will it help?

EW: Has it helped? Has it accomplished anything? I do not know. I am not sure. I write about it in my memoirs. Inside the camp I one day discovered teffilin that somebody brought in, probably paying many portions of bread. Every morning, my father and I would get up early and say the prayers. Today when I say these prayers, I won-der how I could have said that then? It was hypocrisy. It was a lie to say *there* that our God is a God of mercy. There is a sentence, *Ahava rabbah Ahavtainu*, with great love You have loved us, what great love You have given us, and You loved us, and Your compassion was not only great but excessive. *There?* Yet we said it.

ALB: And you did not lose faith there, unlike Akiba Drummer whom you write about in *Night*.

EW: But he did not either. He asked for Kaddish. He wanted us to say Kaddish. He did. He did. Yes. We knew. We saw the smoke.

ALB: A final question about the role of literature, what is hope? You observed that readers should consider Sisyphus happy. Do you still believe this?

EW: Actually, it comes from Camus.

ALB: But I have the feeling you endorse that.

EW: Is Sisyphus happy? Yes and no. Which means that he is not happy. I say I would like him happy. But when he is happy I would want him to be unhappy. But how could he be happy? Which means to accept not this ambiguity, but this conflict in us. Saints have no conflicts. They have surpassed, they have vanquished, they have resolved their conflicts. I am not a saint, nor do we believe in saints. A human being is not a saint. He always oscillates. I talked about the oscillation between good and evil. Therefore, he is still oscillating. When he is on top of the mountain, maybe he is one thing and then below he is another thing. But he is not the same anymore, except if he forgets and he is down. Maybe he has done it so often that he forgets that he will go up.

ALB: What role do you see literature playing in a culture that seems obsessed by television, movies, and the Internet. People seem to have stopped reading. Are you concerned?

EW: I am not an Internet person, so I do not know. I do know literature today should not be what it used to be. In the nineteenth century there was literature to entertain. Then afterwards, it was to offer knowledge. I think in the twenty-first century the moral dimension should be there, which means it should humanize or at least sensitize the reader. That should be the role of the writer today. I say to humanize or at least sensitize the readers to the subject, to the theme, to the implications, to the hopes of the character or the despair in the story, not to the story itself. If a person reads my books and does not become sensitive to pain, other people's pain, then I have failed.

ALB: Well, you certainly have not failed.

EW: I hope not—not always.

WORKS CITED

Camus, Albert. *Le Mythe de Sisyphe*. Paris: Gallimard, 1942.

"Elie Wiesel on the Oprah Winfrey Show." *The Oprah Winfrey Show*. ABC. WLS-TV, Chicago. 15 July 1993.

Holocaust. Dir. Marvin Chomsky. NBC. 16–19 April 1978.

The Passion of the Christ. Dir. Mel Gibson. New Market, 2004.

Paul VI. Second Vatican Council. *Nostra Aetate*. 28 Oct. 1965.

"A Special Presentation: Oprah and Elie Wiesel at Auschwitz Death Camp." *The Oprah Winfrey Show*. ABC. WLS-TV, Chicago. 24 May 2006.

Wiesel, Elie. "Against Indifference: The Urgency of Hope." Meredith College, Raleigh, NC. 17 Sept. 2001.

———. *All Rivers Run to the Sea: Memoirs*. Trans. Marion Wiesel. New York: Knopf, 1995.

———. *A Beggar in Jerusalem*. Trans. Lily Edelman and Elie Wiesel. New York: Random House, 1970.

———. *The Forgotten*. Trans. Stephen Becker. New York: Summit Books, 1992.

———. *The Gates of the Forest*. Trans. Frances Frenaye. New York: Holt, Rinehart, 1966.

———. *Night*. Trans. Stella Rodway. New York: Hill and Wang, 1960.

———. *Night*. 1960. Trans. Marion Wiesel. New York: Hill and Wang, 2006.

———. *The Oath*. Trans. Marion Wiesel. New York: Random House, 1973.

———. *One Generation After*. Trans. Lily Edelman and Elie Wiesel. New York: Random House, 1970.

———. *Paroles d'étranger: textes, contes et dialogues*. Paris: Seuil, 1982.

———. *Somewhere a Master: Further Hasidic Portraits and Legends*. Trans. Marion Wiesel. New York: Summit Books, 1982.

————. *The Time of the Uprooted*. Trans. David Hapgood. New York: Alfred A. Knopf, 2005.

————. *The Town Beyond the Wall*. Trans. Stephen Becker. New York: Atheneum, 1964.

————. *The Trial of God*. Trans. Marion Wiesel. New York: Random House, 1979.

————. *Un désir fou de danser*. Paris: Seuil, 2006.

————. *Un die velt hot geshvign*. Buenos Aires: Tsentral-Farband fun Poylishe Yidn in Argentine, 1956.

A Rabbi reading from the Torah

Transcending the Literary:
Aggadic Elements in Elie Wiesel's Tales

David Patterson
University of Memphis

Elie Wiesel has affirmed that the Chasidic tales of the world in which he grew up have always found their way into his own tales (*Somewhere* 205). If, as he suggests, these stories form the contexts for his storytelling, the tales have their own Jewish contexts in the aggadic, midrashic, and kabbalistic traditions, which form part of the oral Torah. Those traditions, too, provide the Jewish contexts for Wiesel's storytelling; they, too, are among the echoes that can be heard throughout his tales. "Novelists ought not to speak," says Wiesel; "Their mission consists in listening to other voices" ("Fiery" 249). Images and motifs from Midrash, Kabbalah, and Aggadah hover between the words and float in the margins of every line written by this Jew who continues to identify himself as a Chasid. Indeed, Wiesel is above all a *Jewish* writer. To approach him as anything else would amount to more than failing to understand him: it would be a betrayal of the murdered Jews whose muted outcry also abides between the words and in the margins of his every line.

The point is not only that certain tales from the aggadic tradition find their way into Wiesel's stories; certain figures and motifs from that tradition show up as well. His allusions to Abraham, Moses, and

Rabbi Akiba—indeed, his entire volumes of *Messengers of God* (1976), *Five Biblical Portraits* (1981), and *Sages and Dreamers* (1991)—are themselves vessels of Aggadah. But before examining some of the ways in which Wiesel draws the aggadic tradition into his tales, one should briefly consider the significance of storytelling in the Jewish tradition. In that way one may acquire a better sense of the Jewishness of this Jewish storyteller.

I. Aggadah in the Jewish Tradition

Jewish tradition teaches that the Torah is the blueprint of all creation: four times, it is written in the Midrash, the Holy One looked into the Torah before beginning His work of creation (*Bereshit Rabbah* 1:1).[1] Unlike a blueprint, however, the Torah is itself the *stuff* of creation. This teaching from the Midrash is central to the ancient teachings found, for example, in the *Sefer Yetzirah*, the *Book of Creation*, where it is said that Hashem "created His universe with three books [*sefarim*]: with text [*sefer*], with numbering [*sefar*], and with storytelling [*sipur*]" (1:1). The People of the Book—the People of the *Sefer*—are the people of the tale, i.e., the People of the Covenant of Torah. For, as seen in the *Sefer Yetzirah*, in the beginning was the tale—the *sipur*—and the tale is made of Torah, as much as the Torah is made of the tale. Thus, says Wiesel, "the tale of the Law is as important as the Law. And it is more profound than the commentaries" (*Souls* 187)—where the tale of the Law is the tale of the Torah, that is, the tale in the Torah and the Torah in the tale. Thus, the Torah includes the tale of the Torah in the Torah itself, in the Book of Deuteronomy: the teaching is not complete without the tale of the teaching. Because Moses relates the tale of the Torah to the Israelites, they are able to bear the Torah into the land. It is a tale, moreover, not just for Jews but for all nations. Hence, according to the Midrash, Moses related the tale of the Torah not only in the holy tongue but also in the seventy languages of the nations (*Tanchuma Devarim* 2).

---

[1]References to *Bereshit Rabbah* and other sacred texts in the Jewish tradition will be cited parenthetically, as above.

This is what Jews are chosen for: to tell the nations the tale of the Torah—that is the light unto the nations: the *tale*.

Significantly, the verb *sipur* means not just to "tell a tale" but also to "*relate* a tale." It is precisely through relating a tale to another human being that one enters more profoundly into a relation with another person. In this process the soul is transmitted from one person to another; life is transmitted from God to humanity. Just as the human soul is made of Torah, as it is written,[2] so is it made of tales: when God breathed the breath of life into Adam, He breathed tales into him. Recall in this connection the teaching from the *Zohar*, where it is written that there are three kinds of speech: speaking, saying, and relating (I, 234a). Rabbi Menachem Mendel Schneerson, the late Lubavitcher Rebbe, explains: "Speaking and saying come from the surface, not from the depth of the soul. The mouth can sometimes speak what the heart does not feel. Even what the *heart* says can be at odds with what the man truly wills in his soul. . . . But 'relating' comes from the depths of a man's being" (74). Relating a tale is a calling of deep unto deep. To transmit a tale is to transmit a portion of one's soul. To receive a tale, as Wiesel has said, is "to become part of the tale" ("Sacred" 187), which happens when one transmits the tale in turn: to receive a tale is to become a storyteller.

Thus in his comments on the depths of relating, Rabbi Schneerson goes on to note a teaching from the *Sifre* on Deuteronomy 11:22: "You wish to recognize the One who spoke and brought the world into being? Learn Aggadah, for in Aggadah you will find God" (74–75). Why? Because, according to the fourteenth-century sage Rabbi Yitzchak Abohav, Aggadah is concerned with

> the description of the true nature of the universe and the ideals toward which one should strive. It speaks allusively of mysteries and mysticism. It speaks of ethics and character and human nature. It speaks of purification of the body and sublimation of the soul. These are absolute truths. (246)

[2]See, for example, Talmud Bavli, *Makkot* 24a.

And where lies the absolute truth? In the task of creating a dwelling place—for God and humanity. It is not for nothing, therefore, that Wiesel keeps a picture of his home in Sighet, Romania, over the desk where he pens his tales. Before him stands the vanquished kingdom, where he remains a child who loves to listen (*Somewhere* 205)—after the Nazis' radical assault on the child.

This leads to a further point about storytelling in the Jewish tradition, particularly in the contexts of Wiesel's tales concerning the significance of the child. In the *Shoah*, children were among the first to be targeted for extermination, not only in order to annihilate the Jewish future that they represented but also to destroy the Jewish tradition that they sustained: it is they to whom one first tells tales. Says Wiesel, "It was as though the Nazi killers knew precisely what children represent to us. According to our tradition, the entire world subsists thanks to them" (*Jew* 178–79). To be sure, many texts from the aggadic tradition attest to the importance of the child both to the life of tradition and to the Holy One Himself, whose presence is revealed through tradition. In the Midrash, for example, it is written,

> Rabbi Yehudah said: Come and see how beloved are the children by the Holy One, blessed be He. The Sanhedrin were exiled but the *Shekhinah* did not go into exile with them. When, however, the children were exiled, the *Shekhinah* went into exile with them. (*Eichah Rabbah* 1:6:33)

One can see that the murder of the child is central to the Nazi assault on the Holy One: in the death of the child one also sees Him in the throes of death.

Wiesel drives home this point with devastating pathos in *Night* (1960), where the reader collides with one of the most dreadful of all the memories that haunt this Jewish storyteller: the hanging of a child. In the assembly of prisoners forced to witness the hanging, the young Eliezer hears a Jew next to him asking, "'Where is God? Where is He now?'" And from within Eliezer's soul comes the terrifying reply: "'Where is He? Here He is—He is hanging here on this gallows'" (71). Then, there is Issachar's wife, the woman in Wiesel's *A*

Jew Today (1978), who sees dead children everywhere. "They are God's memory," she repeats over and over (81). That is to say, they are God's memory of people as well as their memory of God. And only tales lead back to the source of memory itself. Wiesel is a teller of tales not because of any literary aspiration or even any artistic endeavor. In his own words, he tells tales "in order not to go mad. Or, on the contrary, to touch the bottom of madness" (*From* 13). And what lies at the bottom of madness? The *alef* that precedes the *beit* of *bereshit*, the word with which the Torah and all its tales begin, the *alef* that is silent or absent or present as silence, the *alef* that harbors the secret of the Divine Name itself, which is the memory of God.

II. Aggadic Elements in Wiesel's Tales

How, then, are Wiesel's tales situated in these contexts of Jewish storytelling? Of all the survivors to write their tales in response to the *Shoah*, Wiesel draws most upon the distinctively Jewish tradition of storytelling. Not only does he weave elements and motifs of Midrash and Aggadah into his own tales, but he has written his own versions of and commentaries on Jewish tales themselves. His retelling of the story of the Golem in *Golem* (1983) is a good example. It is based on a legend about the great sixteenth-century mystic Rabbi Yehudah Loewe, the Maharal of Prague. At a time when the Jewish community came under the threat of danger, he created a humanoid being, a Golem, to protect the Jews of Prague. It is said that somewhere in Prague, hidden away in an attic, the Golem still sleeps. If so, he slept through the slaughter of the Jews of Prague. Or had people simply forgotten the esoteric learning that would have brought him to life?

Another tale from the aggadic tradition that appears among Wiesel's works is more than a tale or a legend—it is the Haggadah, a prayer in the form of a tale that is told and retold at the Passover Seder. In his commentary on the Haggadah Wiesel writes, "To listen to a story is no less important than to tell it. Sometimes it is even more important" (*Passover* 67). To listen to this liturgical tale of liberation is especially important in the post-Holocaust era, as Jews face new contexts for returning from exile to the Holy Land. If the Nazis' war against Jews was a war against memory, as Wiesel maintains (*Evil* 155), then it was a war against Jewish memory of Jewish teaching and tradition and against Jews' memory of who they are. In the post-Holocaust era, more than ever, listening to the tale of the Haggadah is part of remembering who Jews are.

Wiesel's engagement with the Haggadah extends into his fiction, particularly his novel *The Fifth Son* (1985). In the Haggadah there are four sons who ask four questions. The wise son asks, "What are all these testimonies, laws, and rulings that Hashem our God commanded you?" The wicked son asks, "What is the purpose of all this to you?" The simple son asks, "What is this?" But the fourth son does not even know how to ask a question. One's capacity for returning from death to life rests upon one's ability to remember the testimonies, laws, and rulings given by God. It also rests upon the ability to ask the question—not for the sake of oneself, as the wicked son's question implies, but for the sake of God and humanity. As for the son who did not know how to ask, Wiesel notes that Rabbi Levi Yitzhak of Berditchev identified with him, as he would cry out to God, demanding an explanation for the suffering of the Jews (*Fifth* 35). Perhaps that silenced outcry is what belongs to the fifth son. Wiesel also points out that Rabbi Samson Raphael Hirsch read the four sons as four successive generations (34). Perhaps the fifth son signifies the generation that was murdered.

Just as the aggadic tales assume the form of prayer, so do Wiesel's tales often appear in the form of prayers. *The Town Beyond the Wall* (1964), for instance, is divided into prayers, not chapters. In it Michael endures the torture of standing at a wall, just as Jews stand at the Western Wall to pray, in order to save the life of his friend Pedro. The town beyond the wall is Michael's hometown beyond the Iron Curtain, where, with Pedro's help, he returns to confront the Indifferent One, who stood by as Jews were sent to murder camps. The town beyond the Western Wall is the heavenly Jerusalem where God dwells, awaiting the hour when men shall make it possible for Him to enter the earthly Jerusalem. (Can *He* be the Indifferent One?) In both cases "God is imprisoned," as Michael says (10).

To explain the nature of God's imprisonment, Wiesel ends the novel with a tale from Jewish folklore. According to the story, a man once proposed to God that, in order to understand each other better, he and God should trade places, just for a second. God agreed, and in an instant the two exchanged places. But when it came time to trade back, the man, who was now God and therefore all-powerful, refused. Since that terrifying moment, many years, perhaps centuries, have passed. Humanity's past and God's present have become too much for either of them to bear. The liberation of one is now tied to the liberation of the other. Now, in the post-Holocaust era their ancient dialogue has been renewed, charged with despair and dizziness, with anger and frustration, and above all with infinite longing.

If, for Wiesel, telling tales is akin to praying, then as he tells his tales, he faces Jerusalem—the town beyond the wall. In Jerusalem stands the gate of prayer, which for the Jewish storyteller is the gate of tales. Nowhere is this more evident than in *A Beggar in Jerusalem* (1970), a tale set in the time of the Six-Day War. There, the Chasid Wiesel recalls a remark from the Storyteller of Chasidism, Rabbi Nachman of Breslov, who said that "no matter where he walked, his steps turned toward Jerusalem" (12). So it is with Wiesel: no matter what tale he relates, his words turn toward Jerusalem, for Jerusalem represents precisely what the Nazis attempted to destroy at Auschwitz —the commanding voice of the Divine Presence as He dwells in the world. Just as the *Shekhinah* or Divine Presence is identified with Jerusalem, so is she associated with the community of Israel (*Zohar* II, 98a); the assault on the body of Israel, then, entails an assault on the *Shekhinah* and His dwelling place, Jerusalem.

These are the aggadic teachings one must keep in mind when Wiesel writes,

> Jerusalem: the face visible yet hidden, the sap and the blood of all that makes us live or renounce life. The spark flashing in the darkness. . . . A name, a secret. For the exiled, a prayer. For all others, a promise. . . . Jerusalem: the city which miraculously transforms man into pilgrim; no one can enter it and go away unchanged. (*Beggar* 11)

As the site where the Temple stood, Jerusalem signifies the presence of Torah in the world, and Torah signifies sanctity in the world. It is no accident that Wiesel compares the annihilation of the Jews in the Holocaust to the burning of the Temple (*Ani* 27). At Auschwitz the Temple was itself placed upon the altar.

Insisting upon the sanctity of every human being as well as the connectedness of each to all others, Jewish teaching maintains that every human being is tied to the holiness of the Holy City.[3] This association between Jerusalem and all of humanity Wiesel articulates in *A Beggar in Jerusalem* by relating a tale from Nachman of Breslov, a story of a city that contains all cities. In that city there is a street that contains all streets, and on that street stands a house that contains all houses. Inside the house is a room that contains all rooms, and inside the room sits a man who contains all men. And that man is laughing (30). Why laughing? Because, says Wiesel, "revolt is not a solution, neither is submission. Remains laughter, metaphysical laughter" (*Souls* 199). What is metaphysical laughter? It is laughter couched in the name of Isaac, who, like the children of Israel, was laid upon an altar. Thus, the God of Isaac is known as the fear of Isaac.[4] That fear is transmitted in Wiesel's tales.

The aim of his storytelling, however, is not to paralyze readers with fear but to enable them to live—by transforming them into messengers, as happens in Wiesel's novel *The Oath* (1973). In this tale of the destruction of a Jewish community an old man saves a young man bent on suicide by relating to him a tale and thus turning him into a messenger: "I'll transmit my experience to him and he, in turn, will be compelled to do the same. He in turn will become a messenger. And once a messenger, he has no alternative. He must stay alive until he has transmitted his message" (42). And so Wiesel transforms all into messengers, that is, into storytellers. That, indeed, is the task of every human being: to become a storyteller, a witness, "a messenger, a link between God and man, between man and man" ("Use" 82). That link is the portion of the

---

[3]See, for example, *Tanna debe Eliyyahu* (411).
[4]See, for example, Gen. 31:53.

Messiah in every human being.[5] This teaching from the Aggadah is explicitly stated in *The Oath*: "The Messiah. We seek him, we pursue him. We think he is in heaven; we don't know that he likes to come down as a child. And yet, every man's childhood is messianic in essence. Except that today it has become a game to kill childhood" (132). From a Jewish standpoint, to tell tales is to affirm what Wiesel affirms in the title of one of his books, as taken from *Ani maamin*: "I believe with complete faith in the coming of the Messiah; even if he may tarry, no matter what, I shall await his coming every day."

Sometimes this anticipation is silent, as in *The Testament* (1981), a novel about Soviet persecution of the Russian Jewish poet Paltiel Kossover. In order to protect his father's words Paltiel's son Grisha assumes a muteness that shouts louder than any word. If for his father silence was a prison, for Grisha silence was a sanctuary over which he kept a most stern vigil: in order to protect his father's words when the KGB wants him to "talk," Grisha bites off his own tongue (304–05). Thus, he becomes a poet, "not like his father. In place of his father" (17). In so doing, he also becomes, like Wiesel, a messenger in the aggadic tradition. Grisha's father, Paltiel, notes that, according to Aggadah, as long as King David was "composing his Psalms," "the Angel of Death could not approach him" (30).[6] Weaving his tales and composing his psalms, Wiesel shows how to stave off the Angel of Death, who ruled over the Kingdom of Night and who lurks in the twilight of the modern age.

Thus, one abides in the twilight that Wiesel explores in his novel by that name. *Twilight* (1988) is about a Holocaust survivor and scholar of Jewish mysticism named Raphael and his encounters at a sanatorium that specializes in patients who take themselves to be biblical characters. Here, too, is a teaching concerning the Angel of Death, again from Nachman of Breslov. When one dies, the legend teaches, one lies in the grave and waits for the Angel of Death, who comes to bring one into the presence of the Holy One. There is, of course, a catch: in order to draw nigh unto the Divine Presence, one

[5]Yitzchak Ginsburgh elaborates on this point (7).
[6]See Talmud Bavli, *Shabbat* 30a–30b.

must correctly answer a certain question. The question is the same for all, but for each the answer is different. And so the Angel poses the fearsome question: "What is your name?"[7] Thus, among the patients whom Raphael meets is "the dead man," who is afraid that when the Angel of Death approaches him to ask him his name, he won't remember (141). He is afraid because to know one's name is to know the names of one's mother and father as well as the traditions those names bear. It means knowing that one is called by name for a mission and answering to that call. By asking one's name, the Angel tries to establish something about one's being that is intimately tied to one's doing: knowing one's name means knowing what must be done.

Here, too, is a midrashic connection in *Twilight*. In the sanatorium Raphael also meets Cain, the one of whom God asked, "Where is your brother?" (Gen. 4:9) and "What have you done?" (Gen. 4:10). In murdering his brother, Cain murdered his own name and with it the Holy Name. Echoing the Midrash, Cain says to Raphael, "When I killed my brother, it was really Him I wanted to kill. And He knows it. Any fool knows that whoever kills, kills God" (*Twilight* 58).[8] Perhaps that is why the patient who takes himself to be God asks Raphael to weep for him (213). Perhaps there lies the immortality of the Immortal One: He can be murdered a million—even six million —times over. If children are God's memory, as Issachar's wife maintains (Wiesel *Jew* 81), perhaps that is what must be remembered.

Memory, in fact, is the defining theme of Wiesel's next novel, *The Forgotten* (1992). It is about a Holocaust survivor named Elhanan, who in the throes of Alzheimer's Disease must transmit his memory to his child Malkiel before it escapes him. Wiesel writes, "It is memory that connects [a Jew] to Abraham, Moses, and Rabbi Akiba" (71), a connection Wiesel maintains by weaving Midrash and Aggadah—the tales of Abraham, Moses, and Rabbi Akiba—into his own tales. In this novel he compares Elhanan's effort to remember to a scribe copying Torah (159). Just so, Wiesel himself struggles to remember, a

---

[7]See *Tikkun* by Nachman of Breslov (102).
[8]See *Bereshit Rabbah* 1:11.

word at a time, by drawing the tales that are themselves Torah into his own tales. When Elhanan's son Malkiel asks the caretaker, Ephraim, what he takes care of, Ephraim answers, "What people throw away, what history rejects, what memory denies. The smile of a starving child, the tears of its dying mother, the silent prayers of the condemned man and the cries of his friend. I gather them up and preserve them" (192). Similarly, Wiesel preserves them by gathering up the aggadic memory of Abraham, Moses, and Rabbi Akiba into this memory to preserve what Jews must not forget, if they are to remain Jews, especially in the post-Holocaust era: not only the cries of murdered Jews but the tales of murdered tradition.

If the Jews fall under a judgment after Auschwitz, it is a judgment as to whether they know their name, whether they remember Aggadah, the plight with which Wiesel deals in *The Judges* (2002). Here, like the Angel of Death, the Judge asks the main character Razziel whether he knows his true name, and Razziel answers, "No" (42). Like Wiesel, Razziel is versed in written and oral Torah. Like Wiesel, he has many judges who gauge his every word, including the one person in the novel referred to as "the Judge," who judges five "hostages" caught in a storm en route to Tel Aviv. The aggadic tradition here lies in the very name of the main character, Razziel, a name taken from one of the most ancient of the kabbalistic texts, *Raziel HaMalakh*, or the *Angel Raziel*. To be sure, Kabbalah with its variations in Chasidism is one of the main sources of Aggadah in this novel which contains stories of and allusions to tales of the Maharal of Prague (71), Levi Yitzhak of Berditchev (137–38), Moshe Leib of Sassov (149), and Moshe Rabbenu (183). And, like all kabbalistic Aggadah—indeed, like all of Wiesel's novels—it is laden with messianic allusions. For the Jewish writer who embraces the Chasidic tradition, these allusions are far more than literary devices—they are religious testimony.

III: The Literary Transcended

Inasmuch as Wiesel's tales belong to the sacred tradition of Aggadah, they transcend what is normally regarded as literature. Where literature may draw upon themes and motifs from Torah, Aggadah *is* Torah. The one who tells the aggadic tale does not "author" it—he transmits what has been received. Thus, the storyteller himself enters into Aggadah as a messenger who entrusts the listener with a message to deliver and a truth to attest. Bearing traces of Aggadah, these tales not only show elements of influence from that tradition, but they also harbor traces of revelation. That is why these tales transform readers into messengers in ways that reading *Hamlet* (1604) does not.

Through his tales Wiesel issues a summons that comes from beyond them. Where is that "beyond?" It is couched in the texts and in the prayers of the Aggadah. As seen, these texts and prayers are an explicit part of Wiesel's tales. Even Primo Levi, who turned his face from God in the face of Auschwitz, suggests that the tales of the *Shoah* might themselves be viewed as the tales of a new Bible (59). If this is the case, then there must be a definitive link between the stories of the "new Bible" and the texts of *the* Bible. For the Jews living in a post-Holocaust world, Emil Fackenheim maintains, an encounter with the biblical text has become a necessity, if they are indeed to live as Jews (*To Mend* 18). This existential necessity confronting the Jew lies in the nature of Jewish relation to being. If being has meaning for Jews, it is, in the words of Emmanuel Lévinas, "to realize the Torah. The world is here so that the ethical order has the possibility of being fulfilled. The act by which the Israelites accept the Torah is the act which gives meaning to reality. To refuse the Torah is to bring being back to nothingness" (41). Either Torah or Auschwitz: that is the existential necessity confronting Jews and underlying the recovery of Jewish life in the world, and neither the messenger nor the one who receives the message can avoid this either/or.

If the storyteller is such a messenger, as Wiesel has said ("Storyteller's" 57), then he is far more than a literary figure. Operating within the aggadic tradition, he is a messenger from Mount Sinai who has been plunged into a mountain of ashes. "Let him who wants fervor not seek it on the mountain peaks," Wiesel quotes from the Maggid of Mezeritch: "Rather let him stoop and search among the ashes" (*Souls* 71). And yet there is no *stooping* to search among these ashes, for they have ascended into the heavens to transform the sky into a cemetery. Likewise, Wiesel ascends in order to search not through "literary devices" or "literary imagination" but with sources that transcend the literary. Thus, one may better understand Wiesel's striking statement: "There is no such thing as Holocaust literature—this cannot be. Auschwitz negates all literature" (*Jew* 197). If God showed His face at Auschwitz, as Wiesel has suggested ("God" 309), then one means of approaching that face is through Aggadah, the very thing that came under assault in the Nazi assault on the Holy One.

After Auschwitz, however, this aggadic testimony requires sounding the depths of a certain madness. If the Midrash, subjected to the Nazi assault, is to find its way from the anti-world into the world—if Jews are to recover the Jewish presence that the Nazis deemed an ontological crime—then what is needed is what Fackenheim calls "midrashic madness," a madness that finds an opening for holiness to return to a realm where holiness has been vanquished. This madness, Fackenheim explains,

> is the Word spoken in the anti-world which ought not to be but is. The existence it points to acts to restore a world which ought to be but is not, and this is *its* madness. After Planet Auschwitz, there can be no health without *this* madness. . . . Without this madness, a Jew cannot do—with God or without Him—what a Voice from Sinai bids him do: choose life. (*Jewish* 269)

Through the character Zalmen, Wiesel cries out, "One has to be mad today to believe in God and in man—one has to be mad to believe. One has to be mad to want to remain human" (*Zalmen* 79). One has to be mad, as perhaps Wiesel is mad, to tell these tales.

"In the beginning," says Dr. Benedictus in *Twilight*, "there was madness" (37). In the new beginning there is midrashic madness. With this midrashic madness a Jew must choose life as a Jew, bringing Jewish children into the world despite the fact that the identity that gives them life may well threaten their lives. That is why a Jewish response to the *Shoah* requires a dose of midrashic madness: since

Auschwitz the Jewish storyteller must seek the Word which ought not to be but is, which is to say that the mending of the world requires the mending of the word through the tales of the Torah, which constitutes the world itself, for the world is in the word, not the other way around; and for a Jew the world made of Torah is rooted in the aggadic word of Torah.

How, then, shall one understand this midrashic madness with regard to Wiesel's tales? A tale from the Midrash itself may provide an answer. When Jacob wrestled his identity as a Jew—as Yisrael—from the Angel of Death, the Angel "put his finger to the earth, whereupon the earth began spurting fire. Said Jacob to him: 'Would you terrify me with that? Why, I am altogether of that stuff!' Thus it is written, 'And the house of Jacob shall be a fire'" (*Bereshit Rabbah* 77:2). In the post-Holocaust era these words of Torah ring with new and terrifying depths of meaning, and Wiesel helps sound those depths. In the time of the *Shoah*, says Wiesel, "fire was the dominant image" (*Evil* 39). He answers the fire of *Shoah* with the black fire on white fire of Torah,[9] with the fire that is the stuff of the soul itself. Figuratively, then, to read Wiesel is to burn with him.

WORKS CITED

Abohav, Yitzchak. *Menoras Hamaor: The Light of Contentment.* Trans. Y. Y. Reinman. Lakewood, NJ: Torascript, 1982.

Fackenheim, Emil L. *The Jewish Return into History.* New York: Schocken Books, 1978.

——. *To Mend the World: Foundations of Post-Holocaust Jewish Thought.* New York: Schocken Books, 1989.

Ginsburgh, Yitzchak. *The Alef-Beit: Jewish Thought Revealed through the Hebrew Letters.* Northvale, NJ: Jason Aronson, 1991.

Levi, Primo. *Survival in Auschwitz.* Trans. Stuart Wolf. New York: Macmillan, 1961.

[9]See *Devarim Rabbah* 3:12.

Lévinas, Emmanuel. *Nine Talmudic Readings*. Trans. Annette Aronowicz. Bloomington: Indiana UP, 1990.

Nachman of Breslov. *Tikkun*. Trans. Avraham Greenbaum. Jerusalem: Breslov Research Institute, 1984.

Schneerson, Menachem M. *Torah Studies*. Adapt. Jonathan Sacks. 2nd Ed. London: Lubavitch Foundation, 1986.

Shakespeare, William. *Hamlet*. 1604. *The Riverside Shakespeare*. Ed. G. Blakemore Evans. Boston: Houghton Mifflin, 1974. 1141–86.

Tanna debe Eliyyahu: The Lore of the School of Elijah. Trans. William G. Braude and Israel J. Kapstein. Philadelphia: Jewish Publication Society, 1981.

Wiesel, Elie. *Ani Maamin: A Song Lost and Found Again*. Trans. Marion Wiesel. New York: Random House, 1973.

———. *A Beggar in Jerusalem*. Trans. Lily Edelman and Elie Wiesel. New York: Random House, 1970.

———. *Evil and Exile*. Trans. Jon Rothschild. Notre Dame: U of Notre Dame P, 1990.

———. "The Fiery Shadow—Jewish Existence out of the Holocaust." *Against Silence: The Voice and Vision of Elie Wiesel*. 3 vols. Ed. Irving Abrahamson. New York: Holocaust Library. Vol. 1. 249–52.

———. *The Fifth Son*. Trans. Marion Wiesel. New York: Summit Books, 1985.

———. *Five Biblical Portraits*. Notre Dame: U of Notre Dame P, 1981.

———. *The Forgotten*. Trans. Marion Wiesel. New York: Summit Books, 1992.

———. *From the Kingdom of Memory: Reminiscences*. New York: Summit Books, 1990.

———. "God." *Against Silence: The Voice and Vision of Elie Wiesel*. 3 vols. Ed. Irving Abrahamson. New York: Holocaust Library. Vol. 3. 309–10.

———. *The Golem*. Trans. Anne Borchardt. New York: Summit Books, 1983.

———. *A Jew Today*. Trans. Marion Wiesel. New York: Random House, 1978.

———. *The Judges*. New York: Alfred E. Knopf, 2002.

———. *Messengers of God*. Trans. Marion Wiesel. New York: Random House, 1976.

————. *Night*. 1960. Trans. Stella Rodway. New York: Bantam, 1982.

————. *The Oath*. Trans. Marion Wiesel. New York: Avon, 1973.

————. *A Passover Haggadah*. Ed. Marion Wiesel. New York: Simon and Schuster, 1993.

————. "A Sacred Realm." *Against Silence: The Voice and Vision of Elie Wiesel*. 3 vols. Ed. Irving Abrahamson. New York: Holocaust Library. Vol. 1. 185–90.

————. *Sages and Dreamers*. Trans. Marion Wiesel, New York: Summit Books, 1991.

————. *Somewhere a Master: Further Hasidic Portraits and Legends*. Trans. Marion Wiesel. New York: Summit Books, 1982.

————. *Souls on Fire: Portraits and Legends of Hasidic Masters*. Trans. Marion Wiesel. New York: Vintage Books, 1973.

————. "The Storyteller's Prayer." *Against Silence: The Voice and Vision of Elie Wiesel*. 3 vols. Ed. Irving Abrahamson. New York: Holocaust Library. Vol. 2. 55–59.

————. *The Testament*. Trans. Marion Wiesel. New York: Summit Books, 1981.

————. *The Town Beyond the Wall*. Trans. Stephen Becker. New York: Avon, 1964.

————. *Twilight*. Trans. Marion Wiesel. New York: Summit Books, 1988.

————. "The Use of Words and the Weight of Silence." *Against Silence: The Voice and Vision of Elie Wiesel*. 3 vols. Ed. Irving Abrahamson. New York: Holocaust Library. Vol. 2. 75–84.

————. *Zalmen, or the Madness of God*. Adapt. Marion Wiesel. Trans. Nathan Edelman. New York: Random House, 1974.

At the Thriftway

One night in the grocery store parking lot
I see a woman weeping in her car &
Her engine's running and other cars
Jockey behind her waiting so they
Can get the good spot, you know,
But she doesn't pull out, she just
Sits there with her face streaming

Which I notice as I walk by her car
Because the way she's parked under
The light pole her face is shining wet
Though you can't see if she's young
Or old or anything only the gleaming
Tears. I go into the store to get dinner.
When I shuffle out I don't even look

To see if she's still there, such being
The code of our privacy: we weep alone.
But I wonder, while I am driving away,
If maybe someone tapped on her window
And said *Hey lady, here are some prayers,*
Or, more probably, *Hey lady, you leaving
That spot sometime this week or what?*

–Brian Doyle

White Crucifixion
Marc Chagall, 1938
Art Institute of Chicago

Jesus' Cross in Elie Wiesel's *Night*

Thomas A. Idinopulos
Miami University

I n 1997, Norman G. Finkelstein impugned Elie Wiesel's integrity
about the truth of what is written in his 1960 memoir, *Night* (84).
Earlier, Alfred Kazin also questioned the truth of the experiences
recounted in Wiesel's memoir. Kazin wrote that he would not be surprised to find that the episode describing the inmates who were
hanged had been invented (Zesmer 1). Wiesel responded in his autobiography, *All Rivers Run to the Sea: Memoirs* (1995), by naming the
Jewish victims. In his anguished statement the author did not hide the
hurt feelings inflicted by Kazin's questioning of his honesty. Wiesel
added, perhaps unwisely, that those, like Alfred Kazin, who question
the truth of his memoir join the ranks of Holocaust deniers (335–37).

The controversy between Kazin and Wiesel, one attacking and
the other counter-attacking, continues. Meanwhile, readers are left
with the memorable scene recounted in *Night* of the three hanged
Jews, one of them a boy:

> The SS seemed more preoccupied, more disturbed than
> usual. To hang a boy in front of thousands of spectators was no
> light matter. The head of the camp read the verdict. All eyes

were on the child. He was lividly pale, almost calm, biting his lips. The gallows threw its shadow over him. . . .

The three victims mounted together onto the chairs.

The three necks were placed at the same moment within the nooses.

"Long live liberty!" cried the two adults.

But the child was silent.

"Where is God? Where is He?" someone behind me asked.

At a sign from the head of the camp, the three chairs tipped over.

Total silence throughout the camp. On the horizon, the sun was setting.

"Bare you heads!" yelled the head of the camp. His voice was raucous. We were weeping.

"Cover your heads!"

Then the march past began. The two adults were no longer alive. Their tongues hung swollen, blue-tinged. But the third rope was still moving; being so light, the child was still alive. . . .

For more than half an hour he stayed there, struggling between life and death, dying in slow agony under our eyes. And we had to look him full in the face. He was still alive when I passed in front of him. His tongue was still red, his eyes not yet glazed.

Behind me, I heard the same man asking:

"Where is God now?"

And I heard a voice within me answer him:

"Where is He? Here He is—He is hanging here on this gallows." (75–76)

Is the scene fact or fiction? Did Wiesel consciously (or unconsciously) employ the image of Christ's cross in it?

The Holocaust *ought* to make a difference to Christians in their fundamental beliefs about sin and redemption and Jesus Christ. The soteriological significance of the Christian religion is sharpened to a deadly point when one admits the historical evolution of traditional Christian anti-Judaism into modern racial anti-Semitism, an evolution of which the consequence ultimately and finally was the Holocaust.

Of course, it could be argued that anti-Semitism attaches not to Christian faith *per se* but rather to a group of individuals who, lacking love and derelict in their duty *as Christians*, proved faithless to their lord, Jesus Christ. But this argument can be taken only so far. If Christianity possesses integrity of faith, an inner unity of belief and practice, then the Christian, precisely *as a Christian*, is morally and intellectually obligated to answer the question: what difference does the Holocaust make to one's faith in Jesus Christ? When in the first century Paul carried the message of Jesus out of Jerusalem to the gentile peoples of Asia Minor, he, as a Jew, was convinced of its truth and believed that if his fellow Jews did not then accept that truth, they would eventually do so. Now, almost two thousand years after Paul, Christians should reflect on the truth of the gospel, not in spite of, but because of Auschwitz.

This is more easily said than done, however. The trouble is that with few exceptions the Holocaust is seen by Christians as a particularly Jewish subject, not just because so many Jews were involved in the event, but in a deeper more troubling sense: whatever questions the Holocaust raises, whatever institutions, values, beliefs are to be re-examined in its aftermath are matters about which only Jews should concern themselves. Given this attitude, one should recognize the ordinary, inescapable element of human indifference; one really does not weep over the suffering and death that only touch others. But such indifference also suggests the deep difficulty Christianity meets in confronting the worst disaster in Jewish history, indeed the worst disaster in universal human history.

Paul in his letter to the Romans writes that "God commendeth his love toward us, in that, while we were yet sinners, Christ died for us," and concludes, "Much more then, being now justified by his blood, we shall be saved from wrath through him" (5:8–9). Paul was among the first followers of the Nazarene to proclaim the conquest of sin in and through Jesus Christ. Unquestionably, his statement of belief here defined subsequent Christian thinking. The Passion narratives of the Synoptic Gospels were decisively influenced by Paul's view of the cross's victory over sin and death, and this theme of victory is raised to a majestic level in the prologue to the Gospel of John where Jesus Christ is equated with the Word of God:

> In the beginning was the Word, and the Word was with God, and the Word was God. The same was in the beginning with God. All things were made by him; and without him was not any thing made that was made. In him was life; and the life was the light of men. And the light shineth in darkness; and the darkness comprehended it not. (1:1–5)

The Christian's belief that God was in Christ means that the world's sinful downfall was overcome even before the world began, for "the light shineth in darkness; and the darkness" has never quenched it.

The triumph of the cross over sin and death is sealed by the evidence of the empty tomb, faith's expression of God's miraculous resurrection of the crucified Jesus. For this reason the Gospel narratives became *evangelion*, the "good news."

However differently the various theological traditions of Christianity have interpreted the victory of the cross, it is this message of accomplished redemption that gives essential and abiding form to the Christian faith. And with that message Christian theologians are confronted with extraordinarily painful questions: how could sin appear in the world after the death and resurrection of Jesus Christ; why has human history occurred as it has; and how should one bring the sin, suffering, and evil of the past two thousand years in line with one's theological commitment to the victorious cross? Before searching for answers to these terrifying questions, consider how some great modern Christian thinkers have struggled to provide their own responses.

First, Henry Nelson Wieman, the distinguished American philosopher of religion who taught for many years at the University of Chicago Divinity School, sought to reconcile his own keen sense of the brutality of history with the message of accomplished redemption. He discovered what he believed to be an appropriate analogy from World War II, arguing in *The Source of Human Good* (1946) that Christ's defeat of sin was like the Russians' defeat of the Germans at Stalingrad: there would be more fighting, but the decisive battle had been won, the tide of history had turned. Would that it were true! It would be good to believe that history is a great war where Christ can and did win the decisive battle over sin. But if history shows anything, it shows that Christ did not win but rather lost the decisive battle, not once, but over and over again.

Karl Löwith, the German existentialist philosopher, in his brilliant study, *Meaning in History* (1949), makes this point in detail:

> As a history of the world, the empirical history after Christ is qualitatively not different from the history before Christ if judged from either a strictly empirical or a strictly Christian viewpoint. History is, through all the ages, a story of action and suffering, of power and pride, of sin and death. In its profane appearance it is a continuous repetition of painful miscarriages and costly achievement which end in ordinary failure—from Hannibal to Napoleon and the contemporary leaders.

He adds:

> There never has been and never will be an immanent solution of the problem of history, for man's historical experience is one of steady failure. Christianity, too, as a historical *world* religion, is a complete failure. The world is still as it was in the time of Alaric; only our means of oppression and destruction (as well as of reconstruction) are considerably improved and are adorned with hypocrisy. (190)

But if the coming of Christ and the work of Christianity have not materially reduced the world's sinfulness, what can one make of Paul's faith in Christ's victory over sin? Löwith senses the problem. Like Wieman, Löwith also wants to interpret the appearance of Jesus Christ as an actual revelation of grace, which historically anticipates the complete redemption of man awaited in the End-Time. He regards the relationship between the good that Christ brings and its failure to defeat the powers of evil as paradoxical, ambiguous, a spiritual-cosmic struggle, both visible and invisible. Löwith writes:

> Since Christ these (evil) powers are already subjected and broken, but nevertheless remain powerfully alive. Invisibly, history has fundamentally changed; visibly, it is still the same, for the Kingdom of God is already at hand, and yet, as an *eschaton*, still to come. This ambiguity is essential to all history after Christ: the time is already fulfilled and yet not consummated. (191)

Löwith solves the problem presented by a Christ who came to redeem a history that remains manifestly unredeemed by appeal to a God who, when he chooses, will replace history with a transcendent Kingdom. Thus, what begins in his thinking with a realistic perception of the tragedy of human history ends with the conventional rhetoric of special Christian pleading: what sense does it make to speak of "(evil) powers . . . subjected and broken, but [still] . . . powerfully alive"? If they are broken, then why alive? If they are alive, then they are not broken. Löwith speaks of the "ambiguity . . . essential to all history after Christ." But does the ambiguity lie in history or in the struggles of Christian theology to find meaning in the wretchedness of human history in relation to belief in the victory of Jesus Christ over sin and death.

The conclusion necessarily reached is that Christian belief in the victory of Christ's cross is *a priori* truth, a formal, not empirical truth, a truth established independently of history, faithfully adhered to as "true belief" apart from the factual evidence of history. Holding to such "true belief" leads Christians to a homogenized picture of sin, a flattening out of the experience of guilt. When it is claimed that Christ died for all human beings, whatever their sins, however great or small, then little attention is paid to sins themselves; no degree is allowed in human culpability, no perception of the magnitude of guilt. How very different the medieval symbol of purgatory, which was an insightful, if vengeful, acknowledgment of the differences in wickedness. Martin Luther and the Reformers allowed for no degree of sinfulness. Led by Paul's words, "all have sinned and come short of the glory of God" (Rom. 3:23), they did away with differences. The liberalization and secularization of modern western culture completed the process begun in the sixteenth century by going one step further and doing away with sin itself.

Against this brief overview, is the scene of the hanged boy in Wiesel's *Night* fact or fiction? Whether Wiesel consciously employed images from the story of Christ's crucifixion to tell his own story perhaps does not matter. The same formal elements are there: three Jews, each accused of crimes, one a youth and the symbol of inno-cence—all forsaken by God. Some Christian theologians interpret this story as a Jewish vindication of the Christian belief in salvation through Christ's cross; it also may be a parody of the Christian teaching of the cross. Christians do not teach the cross without also teaching the empty tomb. The Christian story of the cross ends not in defeat but in victory, in resurrection. But there is no empty tomb in Wiesel's story, no resurrection; the story of his cross ends not in new life but with more death.

Christians are exhorted to fashion their faith after Paul's words to the Christian converts of Corinth: "if Christ be not raised, your faith is vain; ye are yet in your sins" (1 Cor. 15:17). But what should the Christian believe about Christ when in the twentieth century millions of Jews are put to death and not one rises again? There is an elemen-tary question of justice here. The real problem with Christian teach-ing of the resurrection is not scientific—"Can it happen?"—but rather moral—"What difference has it made?" Indeed, if one turns Paul's statement around and begins with the ineffectuality of Christian faith through history, one must conclude that men and women are still very much in sin, and Christ did not defeat death. Few can read *Night* with-out feeling that the time has long since passed when one could accept the cross as the symbol of healing through sacrifice, of restoring the order of things by the shedding of innocent blood. After Auschwitz the meaning of sacrificial atonement for Christians has lost its credi-bility. One recognizes that the experience of suffering can reveal a truth that is otherwise hidden. But when suffering, as in the destruc-tion of European Jewry, vastly exceeds the human limit, then dark-ness replaces light, and truth in swallowed up by emptiness.

What Wiesel's story teaches is that if God and man wait to be reconciled and the world made whole by the blood of a young innocent Jew in the twentieth century, as in the first century, perhaps salvation is not worth the cost. Dostoevsky understood this: in *The Brothers Karamozov* (1880), Ivan says to his younger brother Alyosha, "I renounce the higher harmony altogether. It's not worth the tears of . . . one tortured child" (290).

If Wiesel's story is a parody of the Christian theology of the victorious cross, it is also a penetrating insight into the perennial truth of the cross, for each day of the earth's history countless, unnamed human beings suffer their crosses unwillingly and die without hope. The New Testament Evangelists wrote of the empty tomb because they sincerely believed that Jesus was the Messiah, who upon his death rose to heaven to sit on the right hand of the Father. But in telling their story they did not overlook the deepest, most human episodes in Christ's Passion. They describe the scene in Gethsemane where, as the hour of tribulation approaches, Jesus' faith is for the first time crossed with desperation, and he implores the Lord, "Abba, Father, all things *are* possible unto thee; take away this cup from me" (Mark 14:36; cf. Matt. 26:39 and Luke 22:42). Here is a powerful symbol of the common truth that no human being chooses his cross gladly but rather suffers it in humiliation and defeat. The Gospel writers knew that every cross is suffered alone. Peter, who was closest to Jesus, denies his master three times, and all the disciples flee the scene of Jesus' arrest in mortal fear for their own lives. Finally, Jesus on the cross speaks the words of universal human dereliction taken from Psalm 22 (vs. 1): "My God, my God, why hast thou forsaken me?" (Matt. 23:46; cf. Mark 15: 34).

No Christian artist expressed this truth of dereliction more powerfully than Matthias Gruenewald, the sixteenth-century German painter, in two depictions of Christ on the cross: his *Crucifixion* for the Isenheim Altarpiece and a second painting, also titled *Crucifixion*, for the Tauberbischofsheim Altarpiece. The ashen, bruised, dislocated bones, the open mouth of pain, the elongated, skeletal fingers supplicating the silent heaven force one to see a pitiful, broken man alone on the cross, subjected to final punishment, a true picture of innocent, unredeemed suffering. Emil Fackenheim suggests that it was precisely this true picture of Jesus' torment that aroused Christian animosity against Jews as "Christ-killers," not the idealized pictures of the cross where the body of Christ is transfigured, glorified in the imagery of the resurrection.[1] To appreciate Fackenheim's point within the tradition of crucifixion art, one has only to compare the terrifying Gruenewald pictures with Salvador Dali's *Christ of St. John of the Cross*, a masterpiece in its style, in which the Christian belief in the victory of the cross is fueled by the sight of Christ's body, full and sensuous, luminous with promise of new life, fixed on a cross which towers majestically over the world.

The terrible paradox in Jewish-Christian relations throughout history is that often the false story of the cross had to be told to safeguard Jews from the contempt of Christians. The true story is that of human dereliction. The same common human cry of dereliction is expressed in Wiesel's story of the hanged boy who symbolizes each Holocaust victim. Thus, Wiesel expresses a truth of the New Testament seldom seen by its Christian readers—that the Jew who died on a cross in Roman Palestine portended the fate of Jews and countless other human beings in succeeding centuries. Paul employs the language of Temple sacrifice when he states his belief in the redemption Jesus wrought through the shedding of his blood: "Christ Jesus: Whom God hath set forth to be a propitiation through faith in his blood" (Rom. 3:24–25). But if, as Wiesel's story suggests, the sacrifice was in vain, if Christ's blood produces not new human life but more Jewish blood, has any redemption taken place? And if no redemption, no reconciliation between God and man, has occurred, what price in truth do Christians pay to sustain their religion? This is the question Christians are bidden to ponder in their faith, both for themselves and for their different churches, now in this day the light of which continues to be shed by the fires of the Holocaust.

---

[1]Fackenheim asserted this in the discussion following my presentation of "Was the Cross Triumphant over Sin at Death? The Question for Christians after the Holocaust," given at "Confronting the Holocaust: The Impact of Elie Wiesel," a conference held on Long Island in 1978.

WORKS CITED

Dali, Salvador. *Christ of St. John of the Cross*. St. Mungo Museum of Religious Life and Art, Glasgow.

Dostoevsky, Fyodor. *The Brothers Karamazov*. 1880. Trans. Constance Garnett. New York: Modern Library, 1950.

Finkelstein, Norman G. "Daniel Jonah Goldhagen's 'Crazy' Thesis: A Critique of Hitler's Willing Executioners." *New Left Review* 224 (July/August 1997): 39–87.

Gruenewald, Matthias. *Crucifixion*. Kuntshalle, Karlesrude, Germany.

———. *Crucifixion*. Musée d' Unterlinden, Comar, France.

Löwith, Karl. *Meaning in History*. Chicago: U of Chicago P, 1949.

Wieman, Henry Nelson. *The Source of Human Good*. Carbondale: Southern Illinois UP, 1946.

Wiesel, Elie. *All Rivers Run to the Sea: Memoirs*. Trans. Marion Wiesel. New York: Alfred A. Knopf, 1995.

———. *Night*. 1960. Trans. Stella Rodway. New York: Avon, 1971.

Zesmer, David M. "Not Quite an Icon." *Chicago Tribune*. 31 Dec. 1995, sec. 14: 1–2.

In the Historic Cemetery in Hillsborough, NC

I will cling to the rugged cross

Scorning nearby trees and the eaves
and belfry of the colonial church,

a swarm of hornets built a nest beneath
the left arm of Sally Nash's pitted cross,

ninety degrees of slim protection.
Gray as the century-stained stone,

the swirling-still paper layers
are home to the thread-waisted hornets

humming praises to creation,
their steadfast grasp shaming me.

–Eric A. Weil

Bialowieza Forest National Park, Poland

"The past became the present": Reenactments of Trauma in Elie Wiesel's *The Gates of the Forest*

Victoria Aarons
Trinity University

There is a scene to which some always return when they think about Elie Wiesel's work, and that is a moment in his novel *The Gates of the Forest* (1966) in which a Jewish boy in hiding from the Nazis is forced to assume the role of Judas in a town play. It is a stunning moment in the novel when all other action fades into the background, and the specific conditions and instance of the play seem to become the novel's reason for existing. This strategy of condensation speaks to an impulse in virtually all of Wiesel's work: a distillation of events and experience in which the actions that have shaped the narrative's unfolding fall away and become the backdrop for the isolated, circumscribed scene that is now at center stage, a theatrical act that crystallizes a particular instant and anticipates events that will follow. In *The Gates of the Forest* this singular focused moment is, in fact, a staged scene that exists in and of itself, a play within a play.

When the child, Gregor, walks onto the stage upon which he is to assume the role of Judas, the conditions are established for the kind of doubling of personae that will govern the action on the stage. Here, Wiesel crafts a set of conditions that are so overpowering that they create the illusion of spatial immediacy—a kind of myopic centrality, not unlike a telescopic lens blocking out everything that is outside the framed, bracketed experience of the play. These are very visual scenes in which one's field of vision, like that of the characters themselves, is limited to the stage upon which the action that one can only apprehensively anticipate will erupt. Wiesel creates a pinpoint of narrative visualization in which one is trapped, encased in the horror of the experience that will take place and that will take one back in time. Such scenes exist outside of the already established narrative space, where developing, unfolding time is arrested, narrative movement frozen, and proximate conditions encased in a history so overshadowing that they eclipse, at least within the frame of the scene, all other motivations, conceits, and characterizations. In the play within a play in *The Gates of the Forest*, there is a reordering, a restructuring of time in which "the past became the present" (58). The present no longer unfolds from the past but regresses into its motivational depths. This particular and powerful moment, which can be taken as paradigmatic of Wiesel's fiction, constitutes less a circling back in time than the production of a kind of stasis that transforms time, place, and identity as it reenacts past trauma.

The Gates of the Forest is the story of Gregor, a young Hungarian Jew in hiding from the Nazis. He takes refuge in the forests, finally seeking shelter at the home of his old family servant Maria, a gentile who risks her life to save him. In order to protect him from the presumptive and accurate knowledge among the villagers that he is a Jew, she introduces Gregor as her deaf and mute nephew, the son of her sister Ileana, who long before left the village in disgrace. Gregor is provided with a new identity, "a home, a past, a story" (64). In this remote village in Romania, where Gregor is something of a curiosity, the villagers are smug and self-satisfied, living in isolation from cultural life beyond the confines of the village. To these peasants, "a deaf-mute was not dangerous" (70). Indeed, Gregor's feigned condition gives them surprising license to confide in him their secret desires and their transgressions. Gregor is their confessor but a priest who can give neither penance nor absolution since he can neither hear nor speak. He is silenced by the war, in hiding and in disguise.

It is a village out of time, save for existing against the backdrop of
Nazi occupation and death camps. As Wiesel puts it, "somewhere,
in the distance, there was a war" (95).

When Gregor is cast as Judas in the annual school play, the
"timely subject" of which is "the Jews, or more precisely, hatred of
the Jews and its justification," an idea inspired by the teacher's "over-
flowing enthusiasm and imagination" (88), the war is pushed to center stage. It is an ancient war against the Jews, inflamed by "an
ancient hate, suddenly reawakened," and Gregor knows, just as
surely as he believes his own death is upon him, that "at a single
word these people would have marched backwards through time to
add another cross to those of Golgotha" (103). It is significant that
Gregor not only plays the role of Judas, but that he is also a silent
and undefended Judas. And here, Gregor as Judas functions as a
metonym for the Holocaust; the entire scene, in fact, is a met-
onymic representation of the massacre of Jews with the villagers as
all-too-willing persecutors.

For when Gregor enters at center stage, "a silent Judas," the perfect casting for "a Judas struck dumb by God," the villagers readily
and eagerly forget that he is the deaf-mute nephew of their neighbor,
Maria (89). Significantly, the village is located in a remote landscape, far from the immediate dangers of the cities where Nazis are
rounding up and deporting Jews. But the dangers are equally great in
this isolated village, for its very seclusion, its inaccessibility, and its
obscurity take it out of time. The village becomes a mythic place
and, as such, accountable to no outside, intrusive influences nor
structures; it is, then, only accountable to its own, thus making it accountable to none. But, although the novel has aspects of fantasy,
this is not a fairy tale, for in "real time" the war against Jews, the destruction and obliteration of Eastern European Jewry by the Nazi
regime, locates this village in the immediacy of reality. While the re-
moteness of the village might have created a covering for shelter, instead, the villagers recreate within the canopy of the village their
own microcosmic war of retaliation against Jews. It is an attack bred
of the re-invocation of an originating myth of Jewish faithlessness, its
reemergence authorized by contemporary hatred and annihilation,

and it is here that the imaginary and the real intersect. The villagers' assault on Gregor, the young Jew, is for Wiesel part of an uninterrupted, continuous revenge unmediated by time. Gregor's suffering, as an embodiment of the historical and immediate suffering of Jews, has its origins in myth, which reinforces the repetitive endlessness of suffering, since such conditions live on in mythic time. The hatred and fear of the villagers transform Gregor into the legendary figure of Judas, who stands before them at this particular moment in time, the Nazi war fading backstage. The villagers are unable to separate their own hideous self-deception from the reality of the situation: a child on a stage. They believe, because they so desperately want to, that Gregor is, indeed, Judas, whose betrayal is responsible for the crucifixion of Christ. Further, they must believe this, for it justifies anything that they have done and intend to do.

But Gregor's participation in the play, as Wiesel ironically suggests, remains a matter of representation and interpretation, of fictional construction of character and motivation. Gregor, stepping into the role of Judas, like any seasoned actor (for, after all, he's been donning different masks, trying to circumvent the danger of a fixed identity, all along), attempts to decipher the character of Judas and so better to enact the role. But any such analysis of character and plot makes no sense to Gregor, for the presumed actions of Judas make for a thin plot, lacking in adequate motivation and believability with a Judas who himself acts, as it were, out of character. In trying to decode the playtext, Gregor discovers a fundamental flaw in the design of the legend:

> Who was he? Christ's best disciple and closest friend. From one day to the next, and for no apparent reason, his loyalty was shattered and Judas became a traitor. . . . Why this sudden change? According to the Gospels there was an obscure story of money. Thirty pieces of silver. Absurd and inconceivable: The money adds to the mystery rather than explaining it. Christ's companions had no interest in terrestrial things—these had nothing to do with their aspirations. There had to be other reasons, more hidden than these. If the disciple abandoned his Master for

thirty miserable pieces of silver, it meant that both men were more vulnerable than they knew. (94)

Wiesel's Gregor here takes the legend on as text, that is, as an opening for dialogue and contention.

In Wiesel's midrashic retelling of the Judas story, the motivation for the unfolding of the central act of betrayal, the act that will set in motion the irreparable events that follow, becomes the point at which the story reveals its flaws. Motivation must be seen as the real human factor in any story, since it provides an answer to the central question, "why," and thus to the origins of actions. Plausible motivation, the impetus that drives and impels affect and action, hopes to resolve the ambiguities of character and plot. But here, the authorizing source of the story of Judas's betrayal of his Master and friend gives an unsatisfying and insufficient answer to the question. The proposed answer, monetary gain, is much too rote, too commonplace and conventional, to have any epistemological or psychological reliability. Money, especially in this instance, is far too banal a rationale to explain the fantastic events that it portends. What makes motivation so interesting, so central to the unfolding of narrative, is the exposure of unconscious and thus uncontrollable drives. And here, Wiesel returns readers to a time before the event, a defining moment where motivation might be established. But, as Gregor contends, the explanation of money only "adds to the mystery" (94). The story is, however, the script that Gregor is given. Improvising, then, Gregor rejects the narrative for one of his own. The story of the money can only level the playing field. No longer Master and disciple, both Christ and Judas show their weaknesses and thus are made "more vulnerable than they knew" (94). This mutual vulnerability sets the stage for a reversal of identities: "Judas . . . the saint. . . . He is the victim; not Jesus; he is the crucified; not the Christ" (109). In demanding that Judas be acknowledged as the crucified, Gregor rewrites "history"; he revises myth in order to demand that there be a future, that, in fact, myth will not revisit itself in an endless replay of a scene rewound to the place of its origin.

Characteristically for Wiesel, a changing of roles takes place: "Judas the crucified; not the Christ." Roles played are exactly that, actors taking on different parts as they vie for center stage, and so victimizer becomes victim, and executioner, the condemned. But for Wiesel, this exchange of identities is less a matter of stepping out of one persona and into another than of taking on a real identity. Although Gregor will in his performative act on the stage assume the role of Judas, this is not really a matter of play-acting; it is less a matter of representation than a reenactment of events. Gregor here replaces Judas, just as Judas, "resurrected" for the moment of the play, replaces Gregor. Neither figure stands in for the other, but, rather, in a chiastic move the one becomes the other, just as, later, Judas/Gregor in his suffering will become Christ. Judas, arisen out of myth, and Gregor become interchangeable, a structural and figural conceit that one finds elsewhere in the novel. At the novel's opening, for example, Gregor by mysterious design meets Gavriel, a Jewish boy who saves him and becomes his double, the boy whose "name . . . went away one day, without reason, without excuse. . . . In time of war millions of men live under false names; there is a divorce between man and his name. Sometimes the name has had enough and goes away" (9). In a cryptic interchange marked by ambiguous pronoun reference, the boys merge identities: "He had no name, so he gave him his own" (3). The one boy will become indistinguishable from the other and in doing so suggest the way in which the traumatic event of the one boy's death may be sublimated by the other. Gregor's interconnectedness with Gavriel transforms the other boy's trauma into his own, unmediated by a separation of identities insisted upon by the individuality of names. Gregor in taking Gavriel's name does not represent Gavriel but, rather, brings him back to life by making his life his own and in doing so bears witness to the suffering of others, which, for Wiesel, is the obligation of the survivor. The exchange of names gives voice to the other, and thus Gregor can reemerge as Gavriel later in the novel, just as he can emerge as Judas, the legend as unmediated text.

For the villagers in *The Gates of the Forest*, whom Wiesel characterizes as "the crowd delirious with an ancient hate," there is no ambiguity (103). For them it is not Gregor but Judas who stands before them on the stage of their loathing. For the villagers this is not a matter of representation; it is no longer a play but, rather, *the* place of betrayal and crucifixion and thus the justification for the acting out of their vengeance. The play is less a suspension of disbelief than it is the aggressive promotion of belief. Myth and ritual provide a justification for belief and action. In attacking Gregor, the villagers, to their own thinking, in an act of pathological self-righteousness elevate themselves by participating in a tradition of revenge legitimized long before them: "Neither the blood nor the face were his. They belonged to someone else, 2000 years dead, but kept cruelly alive to expiate the crimes committed by others" (104). Their brutality stems from a guilty projection of their own sins, inadequacies, and failures onto Gregor, for whom all moorings disappear.

No longer are there stable markers of place and identity, no familiar cultural landmarks but, instead, an evisceration of cultural location and legitimacy that characterizes Holocaust narratives. For Gregor, "everything became confused with everything else: beings lost their identity, objects their proper weight" (58). Gregor finds himself back in time, in mythic time, where there is no mediating distance between trauma and identity. He is unable to repress or turn away from the site of traumatic origin. Judas is not "remembered," not even as a manifestation of the collective unconscious, but becomes, rather, a part of an event realized in the present through myth. The past erupts into the present, and mythic time becomes real time. In psychoanalytic terms trauma is the symbolic eruption of the past into the present, a repetitive replaying of a traumatic event (and this is made emphatic in virtually all of Wiesel's Holocaust writing). Cathy Caruth recalls Freud's explanation of the recurring traumatic dream as one in which the event literally returns "against the will of the one it inhabits . . . an overwhelming occurrence that then remains, in its insistent return, absolutely true to the event" ("Trauma" 5). If one likens the play to a dream, then Gregor is, indeed, caught in the literal moment of Judas's betrayal of Christ and the catastrophic events that "inevitably, inexorably" follow (Gates 100). The difference here, of course, lies between the conscious recognition on Gregor's part that the play is, indeed, a play and the unconscious "dream" in which the dreamer returns to that which happened unexpectedly and violently in the past.

This return to the past is complicated in Gregor's case by the fact that the recurring traumatic event did not literally happen to him. For Gregor, it is an imagined event, since the traumatic experience is happening in the present but is motivated by and has its roots in a past not his own. So there are really two traumatic episodes here: the event that exists in legend and the newly felt but historically repetitive trauma that Gregor experiences. But if mythic time is conceived here at least for this moment as real time, and if Gregor, in the kind of chiastic interchange so characteristic of Wiesel's work, has become Judas for this essential moment in the novel, then the stage upon which Gregor plays the role of Judas is the primal scene of an anti-Semitic fantasy to which he is forced to return. It is a replay of events that begins at a point of origin, Judas condemned for the alleged betrayal of Christ. Rachel Bowlby suggests that it is in the "return to the point of origination" through "repetition and re-reaction" that the "past, present, and future interfere with one another and reconnect; a painful 'return' of or to a past, resurrected and relived" (vii). Such a process is thought to be therapeutic, to bring an end to suffering. But in Gregor's case Wiesel makes the suffering intensify and the trauma continue. Ironically, it is not Christ who is resurrected but Judas. It is an unwelcome resurrection, to be sure. Judas is resurrected not in Christlike sanctification but in an attempt to revisit his condemnation, to revalidate his guilt—Judas not blessed but cursed. It is through the conceit of the play that the immediacy of the event is realized, since the stage eclipses all other dramatic action and creates a sense of urgency that begs for resolution.

Similarly, in other moments in the novel the unfolding action is abruptly arrested, and the play-scene intrudes. The illusion of theatrical unreality is destabilized by the narrative's eruption into the performative language of theater. The silence that abruptly descends upon the forest after Gavriel's capture and death, the loss of one Jewish boy that brings the other to his knees in the isolated grief of one stunned by his own survival, closes in on itself. The horror of this solitary death is only a brief interlude, made all the more horrible by its seeming insignificance—after all, it is a "mere" intermission. Gavriel's death and the impossible articulation of Gregor's anguish are pushed off-stage, for the play seems to have no end:

> Intermission was over. The play began again. The actors were
> back on the stage and officers in dazzling uniforms stood in front
> of the firing squads, raising their arms and calling out, 'Fire, fire,
> fire!' And soldiers bored, fired their machine guns, indifferent,
> thinking of nothing, not even of death. (*Gates* 60)

The actors, bored by and indifferent to what are surely ritualized,
repetitive, too often rehearsed scenes, act in a prescribed manner.

So, too, this scene comes to its inevitable and inescapable close,
"the Messiah himself, a thousand times, a thousand, thousand times
multiplied, [falling] into the ditch" (60), the curtain falling, only to
open again, the accumulation of atrocity upon atrocity. There is no
deviation, no improvisation nor rewriting of lines already scripted.
For Wiesel, there is no mistaking reality for fiction by explicit references to actors upon a stage. Rather, the interspersion of the play into
the narrative makes more emphatic the obscenities of the Holocaust
not *acted* but *enacted* upon its victims. The abruptness with which the
play sequences are introduced into the narrative and the fragmenta-
tion and cutting off of one scene only to be reopened with another
create a bombardment of images. The stage isolates and thus focuses
its attention on a particular decisive scene, amplified by its upstaging
of anything else, as if the entire novel is reduced exactly to this particular place and point in time. There is, for Wiesel, no way off stage,
no way to escape the savage endlessness of the Holocaust that extends well beyond the end of the war and the liberation of the camps,
the scenery forever "peopled with ghosts and murderers" (212).

While Gregor on stage as Judas is trapped in the physical, theatrical, and public space of the stage, the psychic space of the projected,
delusional hatred of the audience creates a kind of double consciousness in which Gregor is carried to another place and time through
the villagers' primitive response to his performative act. The scene,
here, is frozen, as is the audience. While the setting of the stage
seems to be circumscribed, its isolation is only an illusion created by
stagecraft. For here, the psychic evanescence of spatial relations
breaks down, and Gregor is no longer separated spatially from the
audience of villagers, who advance menacingly upon him with cries
of "No pity! Let justice be done! Vengeance," their blows executed

by a "blood thirstiness" (105). Temporal space, too, is transgressed. Thus, myth carries with it the possibility of scapegoating in the future, of justifying the Holocaust. The villagers, as they militantly advance upon Gregor, are, indeed, no longer solely an unruly following of lawless peasants responding in hysterical outrage but, rather, "soldiers preparing to assault invisible barricades" (112). They are, like Nazi troops, going into battle as part of the machinery of the Third Reich, sanctioned by law. They are no longer taking their vengeance out on a singular Jewish boy but participating in the war against all Jews, urged on by sanctimonious self-interest, "executioners . . . about to invade . . . and avenge their honor in blood" (113). Past and present hatred escalate, gain in momentum, and converge at this particular point in time, no longer mythic time but the immediate and exact moment of the Holocaust.

As the violence increases, Gregor, bloodied and wounded, transcends the experience, the scene having the "unreal, oppressive quality of a nightmare" (106). He momentarily withdraws from the physical sensation of pain, ironically a self-protective reflex, a response to the trauma of the nightmare from which he does not want to awaken, for to wake from the dream is to experience the pain from which he desires relief. If one understands "nightmare" here metaphorically, then Gregor in the midst of the nightmare/trauma temporarily dissociates himself from the present traumatic experience.[1] He removes himself, as it were, from the experience, distancing himself by withdrawing further into himself. As long as Gregor is enclosed in the parameters of the nightmare, he is not really "living" the experience. But he does awaken; he regains "consciousness" and does so because he wills himself to, "seized by a burning desire to take part in the show and direct it" (106). If he cannot prevent the

---

[1]Bessel A. Van der Kolk and Onno Van der Hart discuss trauma victims' responses to the overwhelming nature of a traumatic episode in terms of dissociation, as being "automatically . . . removed from the scene; they look at it from a distance or disappear altogether." Interestingly, they make an important distinction in this regard between dissociation and repression, the latter a process of pushing the traumatic memory away, while dissociation seems to be more a matter of pushing oneself away from the experience (168–69).

hostility and sadistic violence that drive the villagers to kill him, then he can, at the very least, direct the action, assume some agency in his own undoing, not unlike Sol Nazerman, the pawnbroker in Edward Lewis Wallant's *The Pawnbroker* (1961), who at the moment of his impending death ironically assumes the posture of a "commander of his own firing squad" (268). Curiously, the savagery of the villagers' attack strangely frees Gregor, causing him to step back into his own character and, thereby, to direct the final act of the play.

No longer willing to accept the hostility and hypocrisy of the villagers, Gregor on stage finally breaks his silence and speaks. Indeed, his disorientation and terror continue to escalate until he erupts into speech. This is a decisive moment, for speaking, after all, is an expression of autonomous self-presentation and survival. The irony here is that Gregor's loss of voice is necessary, at least initially, for survival. As long as he does not speak, he can disguise his Jewish identity. However, at the moment in which he becomes Judas in the eyes of the villagers, his silence no longer can protect him. In fact, for the villagers Gregor's silence is proof of his guilt. Gregor-now-Judas has been to the villagers' delight rendered mute by God as punishment for his betrayal of Christ. Silence here, as elsewhere in the literature of the Holocaust, represents a loss of identity, both figuratively and literally.

The descent into silence is a central and recurring feature of Holocaust narratives. The deeply traumatized child in Jerzy Kosinski's *The Painted Bird* (1965), for example, loses his voice as a response to the trauma he experiences; the last sound that he makes before his loss of speech is a cry of pain. Speech is useless to the young boy since there is no one to whom he can cry out for help. His voice only imperils him, since any sound he would make in hiding would expose him, making him all the more vulnerable. Silence is viewed here as a splitting of the self, his voice escaping while he cannot. It is only at the close of the novel that the child regains his voice and, in an incessant outpouring of words, "enraptured by the sounds that were heavy with meaning" (234), is able, if only guardedly and distrustfully, to move back into the world. Voice is the articulation of the self, and it is though speech that one may insist upon self-invention and self-determination. To return to the metaphor of the nightmare, a dream-state in which the outcome of the violent experience is delayed, Gregor thus awakens into speech, into conscious articulation of the pain as he endures it. In choosing to speak, Gregor momentarily empowers himself. It is he who chooses not only *to* speak at this particular juncture but *what* to speak. The words are generated by and belong to him, and even if speech hastens his death by further enraging the peasants, then his death, too, will be his own.

Gregor, his speech regained, "testifies" and thus bears witness to his suffering and, metonymically, to the suffering of others. In psychoanalytic terms, the hope is that narrating the traumatic events or reliving them through narrating the experience will bring relief. Thus in regaining speech, Gregor by way of his eruption into speech regains agency, thereby reestablishing his identity and history: "I'm not Judas. . . . I can't act in his name. . . . I am a Jew and my name is a Jewish name, Gavriel" (*Gates* 111). Having been mute for so long, his voice, once heard, is deafening. In this moment Wiesel creates a kind of still, an arresting of all action, the stage moving outward, encompassing the audience as part of the set, and here the villagers, perfectly cast, play themselves:

> [T]hey froze, incredulous, as if death had surprised them in the midst of battle. Projected out of time they were like wax figures, grotesque and idiotic, without destiny or soul, clay creatures, damned in the service of the devil. Their upraised arms hung in the air, their mouths were half open with tongues protruding and features swollen; the slightest breath would have knocked them over and returned them to dust. All breathing ceased. (107)[2]

The scene is frozen in a kind of suspended animation, broken only by the villagers' cries for mercy that will forever exist just beyond their reach, for they are beyond redemption. Gregor, momentarily having

[2]This description is strangely reminiscent of I. L. Peretz's 1915 short story "Ne'ilah in Gehenna," where the fiends of Hell "stationed at the caldrons," arrested by the cries of the dead, stand "bewildered, abashed . . . faces twisted . . . mouths agape . . . tongues lolling . . . eyes bulging from the sockets" (218).

taken control of what was meant to be the final act of the play, demands acknowledgment of their deceit, their duplicity, and their barbarous treachery. He also demands from them acknowledgment of his identity, the very identity that was at the root of their hatred and fear. In defining himself as a Jew and in taking on the "borrowed" name of Gavriel, Gregor resurrects himself as well as the dead boy and thus bears witness not only to his own suffering and agency but also to that of others, those victims whose voices have been lost forever. Gregor on the stage stands before the villagers as a prophet. Not only does he foresee the future, but he also *is* the future, a future imperiled by the ignorant villagers' reenactment of a mythic past.

The sense of relief and power that Gregor feels in testifying, however, does not bring with it the hoped-for reprieve from trauma, for it is ongoing. As the scene draws to a close, the war, which is temporarily the backdrop against which the play takes place, now regains center stage in the novel, its historical trauma the context for the individual trauma of the Jewish boy, Gregor. Wiesel here contextualizes the individual trauma and replays it endlessly in the wider trauma of the Holocaust. The future cannot be a part of the narrative because of the continuing threat of the Holocaust, and so the isolated frame of the stage upon which Gregor is encased holds him in a particular moment in time and exposes his absolute certainty of the inevitability, if not of his own death, then of the deaths of countless others.

This is a history larger than any one individual. As the play draws to a close, the peasants move toward Gregor "like soldiers. . . . At the same moment, in the crimson fields of Galicia, smartly turned-out officers were shouting the order: 'Fire! Fire!' A hundred Jews, ten thousand Jews were tumbling into the ditches" (112–13). Here, Wiesel links Gregor's fate to that of European Jewry and in doing so reveals Gregor's individual trauma as part of the trauma of history. The young boy's desolation—hiding in the forests, surviving his father's death, and witnessing the death of Gavriel—his humiliation and suffering endured at the hands of the villagers, and his subsequent pain and loss that carry him to the novel's close are not merely symbolic representations of the Holocaust. To be sure, the play in which Gregor assumes the role of Judas and the villagers' brutal assault upon him function, in large part, metonymically: the myth of Judas's responsibility for the crucifixion of Christ makes all Jews culpable in their sinister fantasy, thus justifying the Holocaust. While Judas comes to represent all Jews, so does Gregor, not only in his role as Judas but, implicitly, as one of many Jews persecuted and hunted by the Nazis. He does not, as Wiesel makes clear, suffer alone. Moreover, the villagers' response to Gregor, their persecution and vicious attack, metonymically represents those who turned on the Jews in complicity with the Nazis. Individual suffering is not only parallel to the suffering of all Jews during the Holocaust but intersects it in deeply disturbing ways.

The complexities in such intersection of the personal and the historical intensify the problems inherent in testifying and bearing witness and create in Holocaust narratives an overlapping or layering of stories. "My father bleeds history," Art Spiegelman writes in *MAUS* (1986), the comic-book memoir of his father's experiences in the Holocaust (7). With this epigraph Spiegelman introduces a layering of narratives, characteristic of second-generation Holocaust writing: the history of the Jews in the Holocaust, the father's individual "history," and the ways in which the father's experiences have shaped the life of his son. Neither father nor son can be separated from history, specifically the history of the Holocaust, which has come to define them both. *MAUS* is the story of one man's Holocaust experience, but it is, necessarily and inescapably, the story of the history of the Jews. To "bleed" here is to embody and to suffer the wounds of history. In responding to the implications of compensatory fantasy central to Freud's *Moses and Monotheism* (1939), Caruth suggests that "history is precisely the way we are implicated in each other's traumas" (*Unclaimed* 24). Thus, individual trauma, as it figures in the literature of the Holocaust, is a part of the larger trauma of history, inasmuch as history, the specific history of Jews, is the collective experience of trauma and the defining weight of Jewish identity.

For Wiesel, as for other writers of Holocaust narratives, individual trauma is embedded in the all-encompassing trauma of the Holocaust. There exists, to be sure, a chiastic crossing but also a synecdochal relation between the individual and history, central both to *The Gates of the Forest* and to the obligation to bear witness, a topos of Holo-caust literature. For example, in Wallant's *The Pawnbroker* the inca-pacitating and unbearable experiences and recent memories of the Holocaust for one man carry with them the weight of all those who suffered. Sol Nazerman, the pawnbroker, "with blue, cryptic numbers on his arm" (268), becomes a willing "heir" to suffering, just as Gre-gor, at the close of *The Gates of the Forest*, comes to recognize and ac-cept the indelible condition of his life: the future "mortgaged" to the past. So, too, the nameless child in Kosinski's *The Painted Bird* and the grotesquely fablesque experiences he barely survives speak to the monstrous scope and shape of the Holocaust.

In this way *The Gates of the Forest* through the experience of one boy opens up the historical dimensions of trauma. Similarly, in the short story, "An Old Acquaintance," Wiesel constructs a haunting narrative of a single man's repetitive nightmare of his previous life in the concentration camps, but one that opens itself to the far-reach-ing consequences of the Holocaust as they extend beyond individual-ized experience. It does so in large part because his individual experience was also a collective experience, shared, as Wiesel makes clear in *The Gates of the Forest*, by others. In this disturbingly cryptic story, a survivor's phobic response to individual trauma, to his own anguish and displacement, gives way to the larger, more generalized issues of identity, of judgment, of expiation, and of the nature of sur-vival: "Can one die in Auschwitz, after Auschwitz?" (121).

"An Old Acquaintance" begins with the deceptive ordinariness of a bus on the streets of Tel Aviv long after the end of the war. The bus will become, like the stage upon which Gregor plays Judas in *The Gates of the Forest*, the theatrical playhouse in which recurring trauma is played out. The quotidian very soon gives way to a distortion of place and event. Normal objects are transformed into conveyances of suffocating anxiety, as the bus symbolically brings the narrator, like the cattle cars of another time, back to the camps. The very ordinariness of the opening scene makes the events that very quickly follow all the more disturbing, for readers' expectations deceive them. Also, as in the stage setting in *The Gates of the Forest*, the conditions that drive the unfolding of the story are contained within the frame of the bus.

It is a bus taken out of narrative time, where all spatial relations give way to a scene from the past, the site of the origin of overwhelming events that are revisited upon the narrator, events that the narrator uncontrollably revisits upon himself in his unconscious and repressed fear of them. As the landscape shifts, there is no mediating distance of time or authorial intrusion. Although the bus is slowly moving, Wiesel creates the illusion of stasis, a narrative sleight of hand that directs the interior of the bus onto center stage. The stage set is only the bus, for everything else—the traffic on the boulevard, the city with its lights and its sounds—turns aside, disappearing into the "heavy stagnant heat which insinuates itself into every pore, weighs on every gesture and breath, blurs every image" (116, 112). For the narrator of the story the bus is a place of isolation and entrapment, and, like the stage upon which Gregor in *The Gates of the Forest* is forced to perform, neither passenger can get off.

Riding on the bus, the narrator is transported to another place and time. The sensation of not moving ironically creates the conditions for a different kind of transport in which "the time changes pace, country. The present is in the grip of all the years black and buried" (113). The stifling myopia of the scene focuses on two men alone, the narrator and his imagined interlocutor, all other passengers diminished to the point of obscurity. It must, for readers are taken inside the unraveling of the narrator's psyche in which is played out a dialogue between two men, the narrator and the man from Auschwitz, a Jew, "one of those who knew neither hunger nor weariness nor sickness . . . head of a barracks . . . barracks fifty-seven . . . right in the center of the camp, two steps away from the gallows" (114–16). The dialogue between the two quickly dissolves into an internal monologue, however, an imagined dialogue that takes place in the mind of the narrator, for the barracks-chief, accused by the narrator of crimes of complicity and cowardice, may not exist outside the narrator's ruptured consciousness. The man he singles out on the bus, "middle-aged . . . with a lost look. . . . Easy to classify. Office worker, government clerk, foreman. The anonymous type . . . tak[ing] orders only to transmit them," is the catalyst for his unconscious return to the place of torment and fear (112).

Neither the bus, the other passengers, nor the driver exists for him. The increased internalization of the narrator's fear, which rapidly becomes panic, increases the overpowering sense of oppressiveness, so much so that his own identity is ambiguous, and the one man merges with the invented other. Just as the narrator at the close of Wiesel's *Night* (1960) splits himself from his own reflection in the mirror—"a corpse . . . his eyes . . . stared into mine" (109)—so the narrator on the bus, which is the stage of his undoing, sees himself in the other man, reconfigured, conjured up anew. The ambiguity of the reality of the man on the bus suggests the confusion of the narrator's own identity. Is there a man on the bus whom the narrator recognizes from the camp? Is he the narrator's tormentor, a barracks-chief? Victim? Victimizer? Is the man a guilty projection of the narrator's unconscious and irrational fears? All referents blur; the confusion carries the narrator back in time, back to a traumatic past, back to the site of its origin. The past for the narrator is occurring as if the years separating the trauma of the Holocaust and the bus ride on the streets of Tel Aviv never intervened—"twenty years ago, a tin plate in my hand, before this all-powerful master who was distributing the evening soup to a pack of starved corpses" ("Old" 114). And while the specifics of survivors' individual histories may differ as may the individual expression of remembered events, such characters carry the Holocaust with them; they cannot view themselves outside of the history—distant, mythic, or proximate—that has shaped them. In this way, then, the truth of traumatic experience, as Caruth has described it, is the pathology of history, and for victims of the Holocaust "the traumatized . . . carry an impossible history within them" ("Trauma" 5). The history of the Holocaust is in large part a collective experience and carries with it the equally impossible weight of bearing witness.

The enormousness of history introduces in Holocaust narratives the problems inherent in knowing, in articulating, and in transmitting the events of the Holocaust to someone outside of that experience, that is, someone who did not witness it first-hand. While Wiesel has at times suggested that there are no words that can give voice to the atrocities experienced by Holocaust victims, bearing witness is for him the most central moral imperative that emerges in all his Holocaust writing. In "Why I Write: Making No Become Yes," he suggests that language is insufficient, that words can never hope to transmit the experience of the Holocaust. Silence, then, would seem to be the only honest response to that unreachable place that exists somewhere beyond words. But for Wiesel, like Gregor, isolated in his silence, words erupt, since, as Wiesel puts it, "not to transmit an experience is to betray it" (14). Paradoxically, however, to keep such stories alive through their telling is to keep alive the unspeakable. In describing stories of deep trauma, Caruth suggests that such narratives reveal "a kind of double-telling . . . the story of the unbearable nature of an event and the story of the unbearable nature of its survival" (*Unclaimed* 7). It is through such "double-telling" or double-voicing that survival for Wiesel is made possible. The loss of identity, the retreat into silence, the absence of voice, the erasure of history, the ambiguity of names, the distortion of time, fragmented shards of experience, and such fractured moments as in *The Gates of the Forest* are all characteristics of Holocaust narratives. Ultimately, what emerges from such unspeakable realities for Wiesel is an ethic of storytelling, an obligation to construct narratives of meaning. As Gregor insists, "if speech has been restored to me it is in order that I may use it" (*Gates* 111). *The Gates of the Forest* is, indeed, a story of survival made provisionally and precariously bearable by the assertion of the self through narrative, a survival that depends upon bearing witness to the past, as all of Wiesel's works finally do.

Works Cited

Bowlby, Rachel. Introduction. *Studies in Hysteria*. 1893. By Sigmund Freud and Joseph Breuer. Trans. Nicola Luckhurst. New York: Penguin Books, 2004. vii–xxiv.

Caruth, Cathy. "Trauma and Experience: Introduction." *Trauma: Explorations in Memory*. Ed. Cathy Caruth. Baltimore: Johns Hopkins UP, 1995. 3–12.

———. *Unclaimed Experience: Trauma, Narrative, and History*. Baltimore: John Hopkins UP, 1996.

Freud, Sigmund. *Moses and Monotheism.* Trans. Katherine Jones. New York: Random House, 1939.

Kosinski, Jerzy. *The Painted Bird.* 1965. New York: Houghton Mifflin, 1976.

Peretz, I. L. "Ne'ilah in Gehenna." *A Treasury of Yiddish Stories.* Ed. Irving Howe and Eliezer Greenberg. New York: Schocken Books, 1973. 213–19.

Spiegelman, Art. *MAUS: A Survivor's Tale.* New York: Pantheon Books, 1986.

Van der Kolk, Bessel A., and Onno Van der Hart. "The Intrusive Past: The Flexibility of Memory and Engraving of Trauma." *Trauma: Explorations in Memory.* Ed. Cathy Caruth. Baltimore: Johns Hopkins UP, 1995. 158–82.

Wallant, Edward Lewis. *The Pawnbroker.* New York: Harcourt Brace Jovanovich, 1961.

Wiesel, Elie. "An Old Acquaintance." *Truth and Lamentation: Stories and Poems on the Holocaust.* Ed. Milton Teichman and Sharon Leder. Urbana: U of Illinois P, 1994. 112–21.

———. *The Gates of the Forest.* 1966. Trans. Frances Frenaye. New York: Schocken Books, 1982.

———. *Night.* 1960. Trans. Stella Rodway. New York: Bantam Books, 1982.

———. "Why I Write: Making No Become Yes." *New York Times Book Review* 14 Apr. 1985: 13–14.

Wiesel's childhood house in Sighet, Romania

Elie Wiesel: Second Degree Witness

Ellen S. Fine
Kingsborough Community College, CUNY

I. Wiesel the Activist

Throughout his novels, stories, essays, dialogues, interviews, and speeches, Elie Wiesel has proclaimed himself, above all, *un témoin*, a Jewish writer whose moral obligation is to testify.[1] In his more than thirty books Wiesel bears witness to the *Shoah*, to biblical and hasidic traditions, to the Jewish condition, to history. Although he claims that his works are not autobiographical except for *Night* (1960) (Cargas 62), he has revealed much of his life in his writing. His two volumes of memoirs translated from French, *All Rivers Run to the Sea: Memoirs* (1995) and *And the Sea Is Never Full: Memoirs, 1969–* (1999), are also a form of testimony in which Wiesel is the witness to himself. He defines his project as "a kind of commentary" (*All* 17). In French, he adds "un témoignage modeste, au second

---

[1] An earlier version of this article appeared in French as "Elie Wiesel: un témoignage au second degré" in *Revue d'Histoire de la Shoah, le monde juif* in 2002.

degré" (a modest testimony in the second degree), an expression which curiously is omitted in the English translation.[2]

This classification raises certain questions: what does "second degree witness" mean, and how does it differ from first-hand witness; what is Wiesel's intention in revisiting his life and his works; and do the contents of his memoirs change or add to knowledge of the author as depicted in his writing?

Early in the first volume of his memoirs Wiesel shares with the reader his motivation for embarking on this endeavor. In the late twentieth century there was a proliferation of memoirs by people in all walks of life. Wiesel recognizes that he is part of this generation, dedicated to celebrating memory and its transmission: "I belong to a generation obsessed by a thirst to retain and transmit everything. For no other has the command, 'Zachor'—Remember!—had such meaning," he says (16). Wiesel seems to be referring here especially to the Holocaust survivor's compulsion to testify in "the era of the witness," as the French historian, Annette Wieviorka, has called it in *L'Ere du témoin* (1998).

Underlying "zachor"—the imperative to remember—which structures Wiesel's entire literary universe is the fear of forgetting. In a dialogue with the survivor-writer, Jorge Semprun, he admits: "I have always been afraid of losing my memory. I know that memory is vulnerable. It falls apart" (Semprun and Wiesel 17).[3] In order to combat the forgetfulness of fragmented memory and to ensure a permanent record before it is too late, Wiesel aspires to draw a balance sheet of his life. By evoking faces and events in his memoirs, he hopes to recapture the past, relive loves and friendships imbued with "the anguish and exaltation" of his younger years (*All* 16).

---

[2]This expression, "témoignage au second degré" can be translated as "second degree witness." Both the English and French expressions will be used in this article. The phrase, "un témoignage modeste, au second degré," appears in *Tous les fleuves vont à la mer* (1994), the original title of Wiesel's first memoir (28).

[3]At the end of *And the Sea Is Never Full*, Wiesel reiterates this fear that haunts him, referring to one of his own characters: "Like Elhanan in *The Forgotten*, I am afraid of forgetting" (410).

However, Wiesel also points to some of the limitations in writing this "témoignage au second degré." He has been told that to write one's memoirs is "to make a commitment, to conclude a special pact with the reader. It implies a promise to reveal all, to hide nothing" (16). The use of the word "pact" suggests that Wiesel is acquainted with Philippe Lejeune's work elaborating the concept of "le pacte autobiographique," a special contract between the writer and reader who is allowed to enter an intimate world endowed with autobiographical authenticity. In his book *Moi aussi* (1986), Lejeune speaks about some of the problems that this pact raises, evidenced, for example, by the skeptical attitude of those in other disciplines such as psychology and psychoanalysis. Autobiographical authenticity is questioned, that is to say, whether the truth is really being disclosed:

> [W]hat an illusion to believe that one can speak the truth, and can believe that one has an individual and autonomous existence! . . . How can one think that in an autobiography it is the lived life that creates the text, while it really is the text that creates the life! (*Moi* 22, 29)[4]

Wiesel's own clarification of intention points to some of the same issues and seems to echo Lejeune's concerns:

> I mean to recount not the story of my life, but my stories. . . . Some see their work as a commentary on their life; for others it is the other way around. I count myself among the latter. Consider this account, then, as a kind of commentary. (*All* 17)

A commentary is an interpretation, an explanation. By commenting on his own stories, both real and invented, Wiesel is testifying from another perspective, that of a sixty-six- and sixty-eight-year-old man looking back. The "second degree witness" is one degree removed from the primary source; he becomes witness to his own witness. Afraid that in this process memory may prove to be intrusive,

[4]All translations from the French are my own.

Wiesel warns the reader that he will not uncover everything about his private life, that he will not write a confession.[5] He says he will omit incidents that might cause embarrassment to his friends or hurt the Jewish people. In effect, his memory is selective, elusive, and protective—of others and of himself. "You yourself have written that some experiences are incommunicable, that some events cannot be conveyed in words. . . . How can you hope to transmit truths that you yourself have said lie beyond human understanding and always will?" he asks (*All* 16).

Wiesel thus acknowledges in his memoirs what he has reiterated in many texts—the inadequacy of language. A zone of silence envelops his words. For certain subjects he retreats into the sanctuary of the unsaid. "The unsaid carries more weight than what is said," he notes in *Silences et mémoire d'hommes* (1989) (18). In a key essay, "Changer," in the collection *Paroles d'étranger* (1982), he also says, "I exist by what I say as much as by what is silenced" (187).[6] Wiesel explains in this essay that to convey the shattering cries of the night truly, he would have to publish a book with the pages left blank.

That is why he seeks to explore other subjects—biblical, talmudic, hasidic, and contemporary Jewish issues—in order to protect the silent universe he carries within. Certain boundaries will not be transgressed, for the experience is too painful to confront. The author engages readers but at the same time holds them at a distance. The whole story or the whole truth will not be conveyed.

While the memoirs, like the essays, afford readers a glimpse into intimate aspects of Wiesel's multilayered universe, they nonetheless are marked by a similar reluctance to divulge inner feelings completely. Yet details are disclosed that do not manifest themselves in Wiesel's

---

[5]In *Moi aussi* Lejeune attempts to distinguish between autobiography and memoir, citing the definition in the 1866 edition of *Larousse*: "oppose l'autobiographie, qui est une espèce de confession, aux Mémoires, qui racontent des faits qui peuvent être étrangers au narrateur" (opposes the autobiography which is a kind of confession, to the Memoir that relates facts distinct from the narrator).

[6]The phrase in French is "j'existe par ce que je dis autant que par ce que je tais." See also Wiesel's essay "To Believe or Not to Believe."

other writings. For example, one learns more about his childhood and childhood friends, his closeness to his mother, his special relationship with his youngest sister, Tzipora, as well as his visit to his older sister, Bea, in the displaced persons camps after the war. Although Wiesel occasionally lays bare some of his doubts, phobias, inhibitions, and weaknesses, much of his deeply emotional life remains hidden from the reader. For the most part restrained and controlled, the narrative in the two volumes is at times self-reflective and introspective, but only within limits. One has the impression of reportage in which the author chronologically records events and his impressions of those events, both historical and personal, in the form of journalistic notes compiled from day to day. The author is above all a witness and a journalist. In *And the Sea Is Never Full*, he does admit that his intention is not merely to give a comprehensive account of his life but to scrutinize it, but once again he erects walls to protect his privacy: "I shall omit things that are too private, too personal" (6).

While this discretion permeates both volumes, the books are rendered in different modes. Wiesel himself points to the distinction. In *All Rivers Run to the Sea*, a narrative of his formative years, his purpose is "to narrate mostly that which I see within myself" (*And* 6). He shows how his life has unfolded from a shy yeshiva bochur, growing up in the Transylvanian town of Sighet where he was born in 1928, to a writer and public figure of international renown. The first volume of memoirs ends in 1969 when, at the age of forty, he was married in Jerusalem.

Much of what one reads in the volume has been told before in Wiesel's work. His mother was a highly cultured and educated woman, the daughter of a fervent Hasid, a disciple and loyal follower of Rabbi Israel of Wizhnitz whom Wiesel as an eight-year-old boy once met. Wiesel's grandfather, Dovid (Dodye) Feig, a farmer while at the same time a cultured and erudite man, played a key role in the boy's spiritual formation, transmitting Jewish tales, parables, and songs to his grandson. Wiesel acknowledges that "[i]t is to him I owe everything I have written on Hasidic literature" (*All* 42).[7] Wiesel was

---

[7]Wiesel also pays tribute to his grandfather in "Dodye Feig, a Portrait."

encouraged by his mother to study the Torah, Talmud, Kabbalah, and teachings of the Hasidic masters, while his father, a middle-class shopkeeper devoted to working for the Jewish community, instilled humanist values in his only son.

Wiesel's two older sisters, Hilda and Bea, survived the camps; his cherished younger sister, Judith (called by her Jewish name, Tzipora), perished along with his parents. In the first volume of his memoirs, Wiesel recounts his journey to Auschwitz and Buchenwald, sustained by the presence of his father and then devastated by his loss; his return to the world of the living, the time spent after the war in the Jewish children's homes, Ecouis in Normandy and Taverny outside of Paris; the crisis of faith during his poverty-stricken existence in post-war France; his career as a journalist, first translating articles from Hebrew for a Yiddish underground newspaper connected to the Irgun, then for an Israeli newspaper in Paris, and finally as a United Nations correspondent in New York where a serious accident led to his remaining in the United States and becoming an American citizen. He depicts encounters that have shaped his life: his interview and conversations with François Mauriac that helped launch his career as a serious writer; his meeting with Golda Meir; his friendship with Primo Levi; his brief encounter with Samuel Beckett; the masters such as Shushani and Saul Lieberman who have molded his religious thought.

In the second volume, Wiesel states that his focus will not be directed to the story of himself but his relationship with others. The introvert becomes the activist, speaking out for Jewish causes such as the plight of Soviet Jews and world causes such as the genocide of Cambodians and atrocities committed in Bosnia. Even more importantly, he breaks his vow of being protective of others and engages in polemics by responding to his critics, although one should note that in the first volume he does not refrain from citing those who have virulently attacked him in public, as for example the American literary critic, Alfred Kazin. In general, however, the tone of the second volume is more confrontational than that of the first. Wiesel takes stands of moral certitude. He publicly denounces President Reagan's trip to the cemetery of Bitburg, containing SS graves—a courageous and forceful position that helped Wiesel earn the Nobel Prize for

Peace in 1986.[8] He speaks of breaking off his friendship with French president François Mitterand when he learns of Mitterand's participation in the Vichy government and his longtime friendship with René Bousquet, the French chief of police under the Vichy government who organized the deportation of French Jews.

Wiesel does not hesitate to voice his disapproval of certain works that he feels falsify the Holocaust, such as the film series *Holocaust* made for American television in 1978, the film version of *Sophie's Choice* (1979) by William Stryon, and the play about the Vilna ghetto called *Ghetto* (1984) by the Israeli playwright Joshua Sobol (*And* 117–23). He makes it clear that he prefers documentaries and that a film or "docu-drama" mixing fiction with facts results in confusion and poor taste. He believes that the scenes depicting the gas chambers in *Holocaust* are trespassing on grounds that are "morally objectionable" (120).

According to Wiesel, Jewish tradition "considers death a private event whose secret is to be respected. . . . Auschwitz cannot be depicted; the veil covering this dark universe cannot be lifted" (122–23). Here again, he calls for the same stipulation for secrecy stated with regard to the writing of his memoirs, a recurring Wieselean motif: certain things cannot be revealed and must be left unsaid. Wiesel responds to non-survivor writers who feel this attitude is too "purist." They accuse him of arrogance, of claiming for himself and other survivors exclusive territorial rights to the *Shoah*. He maintains that anyone has the right to treat the subject, but respect must be paid to the memory of the dead. For those who do write about the event, Wiesel says, "I plead for humility, for more prudence, more reserve in both behavior and language" (123).

Yet Wiesel is hardly reserved in answering the critics who charge that he is among those who enhance their literary careers financially by writing about the Holocaust.[9] He is also criticized for being "Judeocentric," thinking only of Jews. He defends his position by

---

[8]In the second volume Wiesel devotes an entire chapter to "The Bitburg Affair."

[9]Wiesel is especially angry at these profiteering charges directed at those who write about the *Shoah* (*And* 124–25).

paraphrasing what he said in his Nobel acceptance speech: "Jewish destiny is my priority, but that priority is not exclusive" (*And* 125). Wiesel's tone grows spirited and even angry when he calls to mind racist anti-Semites on the reactionary right as well as leftist intellectuals who judge him severely.

He devotes a whole chapter to his views on hate, pointing out that since 1988, his organization, the Foundation for Humanity, has been mounting international conferences on the "Anatomy of Hate" which have brought together important figures from different countries to explore and combat the religious, racial, national, social, ethical, and ideological effects of hate's poison. As a public figure, Wiesel has clearly left the sheltered space of the *shtetl* to leap upon the stage of the world's conscience, as is made clear in both of the volumes that comprise the history of his memory.

II. WIESEL THE WRITER

In general, the narrative style in Wiesel's memoirs is rather straightforward as he documents his life. This style is offset by dreams preceding many of the chapters and rendered in a poetic, pensive tone reminiscent of his early literary voice. The dreams reveal his inner self, the self that is hidden in much of the rest of the memoirs. While Wiesel's mother, little sister, grandfather, grandmother, and familiar figures from his childhood such as the beggars of his town flow in and out of his dreams, it is the dreams of his father that frame and punctuate the two volumes.

Appearing in most of the dreams, his father is a constant presence, just as is the father-figure, guide, teacher, or mentor who manifests himself throughout Wiesel's fiction. In the dream that opens the first volume, initiating the reader into Wiesel's journey homeward, his father's unshaven face and lips move with unuttered sounds that seem to convey a foreboding. Wiesel awakens, anguished, with the thought that "he had come for me" (*All* 3). The father draws his son back to his roots, to his origins, to his family heritage, and accompanies him on his journey to the past. "He had come for me" also suggests the author's awareness of his own mortality.

In his memoirs Wiesel often refers to his own books and the circumstances in which they were published. He comments on his works and at times repeats what he has already written, incorporating his speeches, interviews, articles, and stories into the larger picture that forms the mosaic of his life story. He also describes some of the same events and characters on which his stories are based. His memoirs are thus both a continuation of his fiction and a commentary on it.

At times, the stories closely follow the actual situation as it took place, the difference between life and art being barely perceptible. Often, only a slightly modified detail distinguishes the imagined from the real, enhancing the drama of the narrative. A comparison of the real-life incidents as narrated in the memoirs and then transposed into fiction gives insight into the author's literary craft.

Wiesel considers himself above all a teller of tales, a storyteller. When asked what "story" means to him, he responds,

> Story to me is what remains of the event. The substance and substrate is the story. . . . The Bible is a story and story to me is the repository of humanity that one generation leaves for another. And sometimes the same story goes through ten generations and always adds another layer. . . . So when we tell stories, really we do not tell stories, we retell stories. (Cargas 129–30)

In both volumes of his memoirs, Wiesel retells his own stories. A close reading of selected examples from the short stories viewed through the lens of the memoirs reveals how he transforms an event into story, sometimes reaching even beyond that to become a legend.

For example, consider the description of his two visits to the Rabbi(s) of Wizhnitz. The first visit occurs in Sighet where the eight-year-old Wiesel, accompanied by his mother, goes to receive the blessing of the legendary hasidic Rabbi Israel of Wizhnitz. Wiesel recounts how during the visit the Rebbe asked his mother to leave the room and put the young boy on his lap; they talked about Wiesel's studies— a Torah portion, a Rashi commentary, a chapter of the Talmud. He then left, and his mother entered to speak to the Rabbi alone. When she came out, she was sobbing. Despite his persistent questioning for days concerning her tears, she refused to tell him (*All* 12).

It was years later in New York that a relative, Anshel Feig, seriously ill in the hospital, told him why: the Rabbi said, "'Sarah, know that your son will become a *gadol b'Israel*, a great man in Israel, but neither you nor I will live to see the day'" (13). By placing this quotation early in the memoirs, Wiesel suggests that he is proud of the observation and that the bearded old Rebbe's prophecy has been fulfilled.

The second visit is to the son of Rabbi Israel of Wizhnitz, called by Wiesel the "young" Rebbe, who in 1944 was able to escape to Antwerp and subsequently to Israel. Wiesel always had love, respect, and a deep sense of devotion for Rabbi Israel and his son, both of whom were a vital part of his past. In Israel he pays a visit to the "young" Rebbe, now an older man living in Bnei Brak, a religious suburb of Tel Aviv. However, the tone of his exchange with the son is very different from that of his awesome meeting with the father years earlier in Sighet.

The "young" Rebbe (who is never called by name) does not hide his disapproval of the Wiesel persona he sees before him. The secular has replaced the sacred: "'I look at you and wonder who you are. I know who you were but not who you are. . . . And if your grandfather, may he rest in peace, could see you, what would he say?'" (273–74). When the Rebbe asks Wiesel about his work and whether the stories he writes about in his books are true, the pious boy-turned-writer answers, "'In literature, Rebbe, certain things are true though they didn't happen, while others are not, even if they did.'" The encounter ends with Wiesel's wistful comment, "I would have loved to receive his blessing" (275).

Ironically, this unfulfilled wish had been realized in Wiesel's first account of the meeting with the Rebbe which serves as the introductory piece of *Legends of Our Time* (1968). In many respects the details of Wiesel's encounter with the "young" Rebbe are the same there as in *All Rivers Run to the Sea*. Asked by the Rebbe what he does, Wiesel answers that he writes. "'Is that all?'" the Rebbe asks disparagingly, curious as to what Wiesel writes about. When Wiesel explains that he writes about "'things that happened or could have happened,'" that were sometimes invented from beginning to end, the Rebbe reprimands him for masking reality and writing lies. Wiesel replies that "'[s]ome events do take place but are not true; others are—although they never occurred'" (*Legends* viii). This declaration of literary intent is extremely significant and is probably why Wiesel chooses to repeat it, almost word for word, in his first memoir.

Wiesel's utterance recalls that of another Auschwitz survivor, the Resistance fighter Charlotte Delbo, who at the beginning of *None of Us Will Return* (1968) admits, "I am no longer sure that what I have written is true but I am sure that it happened" (128). Such pronouncements reflect survivors' inability to believe in their own life histories. Their stories are so terrifying and extreme that the truth often appears as fiction, even to themselves. Yet, contrary to the Rabbi's misapprehensions, Wiesel does not mask reality but transforms it. Breaking down traditional boundaries, fusing autobiography with fiction, blurring the real and the legendary, Wiesel's works, like those of many Holocaust survivors, defy categorization.

What is striking at the end of the introduction of *Legends of Our Time* is that the Rebbe finishes by saying to Wiesel, "'Come and I shall give you my blessing'" (viii). His intention is to bless Wiesel, the grandson of Dodye Feig, not Wiesel, the author. Ironically, it is Wiesel, the writer, who through his literary imagination is able to endow himself with the blessing he reveals in his memoir he did not receive.

Other stories by Wiesel, viewed through the lens of his memoirs, also provide insight into the author's narrative technique. The modification of one significant detail transforms the real-life event into literature. The first is the theme of the journey homeward which recurs throughout Wiesel's writing, notably in his novel *The Town Beyond the Wall* (1964) and in stories such as "The Last Return" and "The Watch." The pilgrimage to the past is both nurturing and disillusioning. On the one hand, the return to Sighet, nestled in the Carpathian mountains, rekindles memories of a happy life, of family and community where the author-narrator once felt secure. On the other hand, he feels like a stranger in the town that expelled him.

Returning in 1964, two decades after he had been uprooted in April 1944, he gazes upon familiar landmarks—his grandmother's home, his teacher's house, his father's store, the Jewish cemetery.

The dramatic thrust in both of the stories centers around a nocturnal visit to his own house, now inhabited by strangers. In "The Last Return" he opens the gate to the courtyard, preparing to penetrate the interior, but a dog's bark frightens him, and he takes flight, never completing his exploration. Similarly, in "The Watch," the narrator does not enter the house but remains in the yard, digging up an ancient relic, the gold watch he had received for his bar mitzvah. He finishes by reburying this symbol of time past, of the town itself, that cannot be resurrected.

In *All Rivers Run to the Sea*, Wiesel continues to speak of being obsessed with the return to his native town (72). He describes its inhabitants, his family, and his relatives, offering many more concrete details than he does in the fiction. However, in contrast to the survivor's inability to enter the forbidden territory which ultimately furnishes the tension of the fictional stories, he notes in his memoir that "[s]trangers were living in my house. They had never heard my name. Inside, nothing had changed" (72). While the furniture and objects are the same, however, there is one striking alteration—the absence of the photo of his beloved master, the old Rebbe Israel of Wizhnitz, that had hung above his bed; it has been replaced by a cross. In reality, then, as seen in the memoir, Wiesel did eventually gain entrance to the other side. The word "inside," therefore, gives the reader an entirely different perspective from that of the stories.[10]

Another example of a modified detail relates to the last Passover Seder that Wiesel celebrated in German-occupied Hungary in the

[10]In his memoir Wiesel reminisces about his successive returns to Sighet: first in 1964, using his own fictional characters as his guides, he had imagined the return in *The Town Beyond the Wall*; in 1972 he goes back with his wife Marion and an NBC television crew (*All* 361–64); in 1984 he is invited by the Romanian Jewish community ("Sighet" 127); in July 1995 Wiesel shows his town to his son Elisha and his nephew Steve, the son of his sister Bea (*And* 407–08); finally, in 2002 he accompanies the Romanian president, Ion Iliescu, whose government is struggling to face up to its history during WWII, and this time his older sister, Hilda Kudler, also comes with him.

spring of 1944. This final holiday at home before the family's deportation to Auschwitz resonates in Wiesel's memory and is evoked in his story "The Evening Guest," in *Legends of Our Time*, in his essay "Passover," and in other references in his work.

In Jewish tradition a guest is invited to the Seder table. In "The Evening Guest" he is a poor Jewish refugee from Poland whom the narrator's father has met on the street. According to Jewish lore, the prophet Elijah visits every Jewish family at Passover, manifesting himself in various disguises—a poor person, a beggar, a student, an old person, a messenger, etc. "Each generation begets a prophet in its own image," Wiesel reports (27). At the Seder in Sighet Elijah appears as the stranger at the table, the Polish Jew who continually interrupts the Passover ceremony to warn of impending disaster. How can they celebrate the festival of freedom when Jews are being butchered around them, he asks, as he describes the massacres taking place in Poland. "'Pharaoh is not dead,'" he cries, "'open your eyes and look—he is destroying our people. . . . He is alive, he's on his way, soon he'll be at the gates of this city, at the doors of this house'" (26).

The evening guest is the prototype of Wiesel's unheeded witness, a messenger whose futile warnings foretell the fate of the entire Jewish community and who appears in much of his writing beginning with Moshe, the beadle in *Night*. For Wiesel's young narrator in this story, the stranger at the table is Elijah in disguise, but unlike the traditional Elijah, the harbinger of the Messiah, whose role is to reassure, resolve disputes, help people in need, and protect people from harm in the future, this modern-day prophet disturbs and provokes. When it is time to open the door for Elijah—an essential part of the Passover ritual that marks a sign of confidence that no harm will befall those present—the stranger runs toward it, opens it, and shouts, "'Look! There's no one there! No one! Do you hear me?'" ("Evening" 28). He then mysteriously disappears into the night. Clearly, this dramatic gesture is an attempt to alert others that there will be no biblical deliverer to rescue them from the catastrophe.

There seems to be a doubling of Elijahs here—the visible one who manifests himself at the Seder as a messenger and the invisible one who will not come to save the family. At the end of the story, however, the two have merged when, a few weeks after the Seder, the young narrator glimpses the stranger once again, this time marching in the first convoy leaving the ghetto:

> Today I know what I did not know then: at the end of a long trip that was to last four days and three nights he got out in a small railway station, near a peaceful little town, somewhere in Silesia, where his fiery chariot was waiting to carry him up to the heavens: is that not proof enough that he was the prophet Elijah? (30)

The fiery ascension of the Bible has been transfigured or rather dis-figured into a dark metaphor for the crematoria and Elijah into a Holocaust victim.

This last family Seder is also depicted in the first volume of Wiesel's memoirs. At this event the stranger at the table is Moshe the beadle or "little Moishele," as Wiesel affectionately calls him (*All* 59). Moshe was a foreign Jew, among the first to be deported from Hun-gary to Polish Galicia, but he miraculously escaped from a mass grave and returned to tell the tale. No one in Sighet believed his tormented stories, which angered and frustrated him. Thus, he becomes a mes-senger from the dead who ultimately is not listened to (81).

Like the stranger at the table in "The Evening Guest," Moshe in the memoirs is compelled to interrupt the traditional ceremony, obliged to warn the others: "'I would like to tell you what is in store for you. I owe you that, he says'" (60). However, what is surprising in this real-life event is that despite his insistence he is silenced by Wiesel's father. "'Not now,'" the father tells Moishele; "'Your stories are sad and the law forbids sadness on the night of Passover.' We finished the meal in silence," Wiesel notes (60). This is a powerful commentary or rather confession, for Wiesel reveals how the refusal to listen began with his own family.[11] But through the fictional "The

---

[11]Wiesel's father obtained American visas for the entire family but chose to wait, giving away the visas to relatives, Samuel Wiesel and his wife, who emigrated to the United States and lodged Wiesel when he arrived in New York (*All* 357–58).

Evening Guest" Wiesel was able to rectify the situation by allowing the witness to speak out.

The difference between life and literature in Wiesel's universe, as seen, is often blurred, as another example of interrelated life and art indicates. Published five years after the Eichmann trial in 1961, "An Old Acquaintance" depicts a confrontation between victim and victimizer and the interchangeability of their roles, an underlying theme in Wiesel's novels, stories, and essays, and raises important issues about collaboration, collective guilt, and collective innocence, about judging and revenge.[12]

The story takes place on a bus in Tel Aviv where the first-person narrator passes time by playing a game, imagining himself in the place of another, in this case a passenger sitting across from him. When he realizes that the middle-aged bald man looks familiar, the game turns into a trial. Prodding him with questions, first timidly and then more aggressively, the narrator asks the man where he was during the war. With clenched teeth, impassively hiding behind "a mask of indifference, a state of non-being" (43), the passenger refuses to acknowledge that they have met before and says he wants to be left alone. As the tale unfolds, readers understand that the narrator has recognized the former Jewish kapo from his barracks in Auschwitz.

On the moving bus the narrator recalls arguments of the prosecution and the defense from trials he has attended of Jews "accused of having survived by choosing cowardice"—ghetto policemen, members of the Judenrat, kapos (46). He remembers how the prosecution contended that not to condemn the cowards is to abandon those

---

[12]For a study of revenge, see Naomi Seidman's article which compares the notion of vengeance in Wiesel's original Yiddish memoir, *Un di velt hot geshvign* (1956), with the condensed French version, *La Nuit* (1958), arguing that these two books, one written for Jewish readers and the other for a European non-Jewish public, characterize the survivor differently. The Yiddish survivor portrayed by the narrator, Eliezer, sees his death-like image in a mirror in the camp hospital after the liberation of Buchenwald, wants to take revenge, and smashes that image in a gesture of angry defiance.

whom they have wronged, while the defense claimed that the accused were also victims.[13]

At the trials, the narrator experiences both shame and pity for the accused, "gray" persons being judged. He feels relieved that he is witness and not judge (47).[14] However, on the bus in Israel he recognizes he must take on all roles—witness, judge, attorney for the defense. Acting out a trial in his mind, the narrator relives the camp life and the actions of this barracks-chief, how he beat up the old and the sick, whipped the emaciated, gave out food with one hand and struck bodies with the other.

The silence is broken when the two are obliged to leave the bus at the last stop. The kapo returns to his former brutal self, shouting obscenities and threats in German. The narrator, who had thought of himself as the accuser and the kapo as the accused, feels once again like a victim; the oppressor and oppressed roles are reversed. The man whom he had considered his prisoner lets him escape. The powerless one is thus imbued with power: "He let me go. He granted me freedom" (53), the narrator says.

This story clearly contains autobiographical elements, confirmed in an interview with Wiesel by Bob Costas in which the author recounts how he recognized and confronted a kapo on a bus going

---

[13]Primo Levi in *The Drowned and the Saved* (1988), provides a detailed description of these "functionary-prisoners," ready to compromise and collaborate with the enemy and assuming positions of privilege which gave them the power to humiliate those beneath them in the camp hierarchy. As Levi observes, "It is a gray zone, poorly defined, where the two camps of masters and servants both diverge and converge" (41–42). Levi claims that in the network of ambiguous camp relations, good and evil could not always be determined.
[14]In "Une visite en Allemagne" Wiesel says, "je ne crois ni en la culpabilité ni en l'innocence collective; en général je ne considère comme témoin, non comme juge" (119). (I believe neither in collective guilt nor collective innocence. . . . [I]n general, I consider myself a witness, not a judge.) Levi, in speaking of the Sonderkommando, those prisoners selected to extract the corpses from the gas chambers and transport them to the crematoria, expresses a similar sentiment: "I believe that no one is authorized to judge them, not those who lived through the experience of the Lager and even less those who did not" (59).

from Tel Aviv to Jerusalem. "For a few seconds," he says, "I became his judge. . . . And then I decided, I am not a judge; I am a witness. I let him go" (154). In the fiction an important transformation has occurred. The subject is changed into an object: he (the author-narrator) is the one who is let go, providing insight into Wiesel's literary imagination.

In many of his tales there is a twist at the conclusion, an unforeseen ending that endows the narrative with a sense of surprise and compels readers to participate in answering some unanswered questions. In the case of "An Old Acquaintance," readers must decide for themselves what taking to flight truly signifies for the narrator and the author. What kind of freedom is being granted and for whom? Is it freedom from having to condemn the barracks head, to act like a judge and hand him over to the police? Is it freedom from being corrupted by evil and becoming like the oppressor? Is it freedom from the weight of the past? Is avoiding making a decision courageous, or is it a defeat? Readers are suspended in ambiguity.

"An Old Acquaintance" comes into play once again as source and guide in *All Rivers Run to the Sea* when Wiesel uses his own story as a point of reference. He recounts how two brothers, young attorneys from Brooklyn, come to see him in his office at Boston University to ask his advice. They think they have discovered that a respected Hasid who attends synagogue with Wiesel is the kapo who beat their father in the camps. Their father had had the courage to call attention to the kapo's Jewishness, condemning his cruelty for hitting the prisoners while distributing soup, an action similar to the block chief's on the bus in Israel. "'Have you no shame? Have you forgotten you are a Jew?'" their father dared tell the kapo (88). Because of this defiant act, that night the kapo and his aids wrapped the father in a blanket and beat him savagely. One day, in Brooklyn, about forty years after his return from the camps, the father recognized the voice of the kapo.

The sons are seeking justice and retribution. Like the role played by the narrator on the bus when he conducted an imaginary trial, Wiesel now interrogates the two brothers, attempting to determine with absolute certainty that the kapo is the man they say attends his synagogue. If the father was wrapped in a blanket, how could he have heard the person's voice, and could he remember it after all these years, Wiesel asks the sons, trying to cast doubt upon their intense need for revenge.

At the end of this account which in effect is inconclusive, the second degree witness becomes self-referential. In order to persuade them not to report this man to the police and Israeli authorities, Wiesel cites his own story, "An Old Acquaintance," which the brothers had in fact read. At the beginning of his memoirs, Wiesel states that his life is a commentary on his work, and here is evidence of that: "'You know how I acted in virtually similar circumstances. I let him get away'" (89), he reminds the brothers, managing to convince them to investigate with caution in order to avoid making false accusations. Making it clear that he does not want to be implicated in the matter, he even refuses to be told the man's name.

One might have hoped for the second degree witness to disclose his reasons for being unable to pass judgment, first in the fiction and then in the memoirs. Evasive, he keeps his explanations sealed and only uncovers his feelings through self-interrogation at the end of the incident. Consistent with the stance he takes throughout his work, he believes that all Jews were victims and does not want to pit Jew against Jew: "Why did I refuse to hear the kapo's name? Again, only the victims interest me. Are we to be victims of one another?" (89).

Later, Wiesel admits something even more astonishing. He says that he sometimes asks himself "whether I would have been like them had I been appointed a kapo or *Vorarbeiter*. To this day I feel that no one has the right to draw comparisons. Ultimately, the only power to which man should aspire is that which he exercises over himself" (311).

Colin Davis criticizes Wiesel's lack of moral clarity in "An Old Acquaintance." (The memoirs had not yet been published when his study was completed.) Davis believes that the narrator of the story is "paralyzed when confronted with the prospect of making choices" (8) and wants to avoid the responsibility of making decisions. According to Davis, Wiesel's fiction in general contains elements of ethical uncertainty, while in contrast his nonfiction assumes definite positions that convey a sense of moral authority (12–13). He cites, for example, the essay "A Plea for the Dead" as well as "The Guilt We Share," an essay in which Wiesel asserts, "All of us must take responsibility for what happened in Europe. . . . We belong to a generation at once lost and guilty, and our collective conscience lies under a weight of humiliation" (163).

But one could disagree with Davis's notion of "ethical uncertainty" and argue that in "An Old Acquaintance" Wiesel is consistent with the stance he takes throughout his work. He does not excuse nor accept the behavior of the kapo but believes that all Jews were victims. He feels he does not have the right to blame or judge a victim. This may account for what Davis calls "paralysis" and "ethical uncertainty" in the context of the story. But refusing to act as a judge does not in any way connote a lack of moral or ethical certitude either in Wiesel's fiction or nonfiction. Moreover, Wiesel strives to eliminate any variance between word and act. In his conversations with Cargas he reveals, "I cannot go on writing and acting one way and behaving another. . . . Today I demand from a writer a moral commitment as well, a human commitment" (67).

In conclusion, as witness to his own witness, Wiesel grants readers insight into his own contradictions. Humanitarian, voice of conscience, morally *engagé*, Wiesel does not hesitate to take a stand against indifference, injustice, evil, and hatred in all of their manifestations. He writes to correct injustice, to bear witness again and again, to comment on his own witness. He writes to combat forgetfulness. He writes to remember. On a more personal level he holds back from passing judgment, especially on Jews. In effect, this holding back is also evident for the second degree witness who writes his memoirs but is reluctant to reveal himself completely. Elusive at times, illuminating at others, the memoirs mark Wiesel's permanent place in the history of his memory and of the modern epoch.

WORKS CITED

Cargas, Harry James. *Conversations with Elie Wiesel.* 1976. South Bend, IN: Justice Books/Diamond Communications, 1992.

Costas, Bob. "A Wound That Will Never Be Healed: An Interview with Elie Wiesel." *Telling the Tale: A Tribute to Elie Wiesel on the Occasion of his 65th Birthday: Essays, Reflections, and Poems.* Ed. Harry James Cargas. Saint Louis: Time Being Books, 1992. 137–69.

Davis, Colin. *Elie Wiesel's Secretive Texts.* Gainesville: UP of Florida, 1994.

Delbo, Charlotte. *None of Us Will Return.* Boston: Beacon P, 1968.

Fine, Ellen S. "Elie Wiesel: un témoignage au second degré." *Revue d'Histoire de la Shoah, le monde juif* 176 (2002): 50–67.

Holocaust. Dir. Marvin Chomsky. NBC, 1978.

Lejeune, Philippe. *Le Pacte autobiographighe.* Paris. Éditions du Seuil, 1975.

———. *Moi aussi.* Paris: Éditions du Seuil, 1986.

Levi, Primo. *The Drowned and the Saved.* Trans. Raymond Rosenthal. New York: Summit Books, 1988.

Semprun, Jorge, and Elie Wiesel. *Se taire est impossible.* Paris: Éditions Mille et une nuits/Arte Éditions, 1995.

Seidman, Naomi. "Elie Wiesel and the Scandal of Jewish Rage." *Jewish Social Studies* 3 (Fall 1996): 1–19.

Sobel, Joshua. *Ghetto.* Haifa: Haifa Municipal Theater, 1984.

Sophie's Choice. Dir. Alan J. Pakula. Universal Pictures, 1982.

Styron, William. *Sophie's Choice.* New York: Random House, 1979.

Wiesel, Elie. *All Rivers Run to the Sea: Memoirs.* Trans. Marion Wiesel. New York: Alfred A. Knopf, 1995.

———. *And the Sea Is Never Full: Memoirs, 1969–.* Trans. Marion Wiesel. New York: Alfred A. Knopf, 1999.

———. "Changer." *Paroles d'étranger.* Paris: Éditions du Seuil, 1982.

———. "Dodye Feig, a Portrait." *A Jew Today.* Trans. Marion Wiesel. New York: Random House, 1978. 65–70.

———. *Et la mer n'est pas remplie: Mémoires 2.* Paris: Éditions du Seuil, 1996.

———. "The Evening Guest." *Legends of Our Time.* New York: Schocken Books, 1968. 23–30.

———. "The Guilt We Share." *Legends of Our Time.* New York: Schocken Books, 1968. 161–73.

———. "The Last Return." *Legends of Our Time.* New York: Schocken Books, 1968. 110–30.

———. *Legends of Our Time.* New York: Schocken Books, 1968.

———. *Night.* Trans. Stella Rodway. New York: Hill and Wang, 1960.

———. *La Nuit.* Paris: Éditions de Minuit, 1958.

———. "An Old Acquaintance." *Legends of Our Time.* New York: Schocken Books, 1968. 39–53.

———. *Paroles d'étranger.* Paris: Éditions du Seuil, 1982.

———. "Passover." *From the Kingdom of Memory: Reminiscences.* New York: Summit Books, 1990. 147–54.

———. "A Plea for the Dead." *Legends of Our Time.* New York: Schocken Books, 1968. 174–97.

———. "Sighet Again." *From the Kingdom of Memory: Reminiscences.* New York: Summit Books, 1990. 112–39.

———. *Silences et mémoire d' hommes.* Paris: Éditions du Seuil, 1989.

———. "To Believe or Not to Believe." *From the Kingdom of Memory: Reminiscences.* New York: Summit Books, 1990. 23–35.

———. *Tous les fleuves vont à la mer.* Paris: Éditions du Seuil, 1994.

———. *The Town Beyond the Wall.* Trans. Stephen Becker. New York: Schocken Books: 1982.

———. *Un di velt hot geshvign.* Buenos Aires: Tsentral-Farband fun Poylishe Yidn in Argentine, 1956.

———. "Une visite en Allemagne." *Silences et mémoire d'hommes.* Paris: Éditions du Seuil, 1989. 117–21.

———. "The Watch." *One Generation After.* New York: Bard Books/Avon, 1972. 80–86.

Wieviorka, Annette. *L'Ere du témoin.* Paris: Plon, 1998.

Wishful Thinking

To avoid you I go to the toilet,
push dust around the cellar, swipe the slick decay
of leaves from the gutter. Nothing revolts you.
You're so bored you're falling out of the sky
but persistent as sleet,
not like myself whose Bible stops at January,
page-a-day saved by inertia from Easter.

Sometimes you ask me to lie down in the middle of haste
like a madman's blanket. Before how many doorways
will I be thrown down?
Sometimes at dawn I climb the rope with monkey hands
up past fear and gravity, beyond hoarding myself.
An animal knows how much it can take.
I hoist the weights like a rower, one and the other and one.
Don't tell me yet what trial this is training for.

You're the pillow under my head
and over it. You're the hole in the road
that the gas truck hits, jacknifing into gorgeous flame.
The woods above the highway are dark with bears.
A lost child sees the glow, stumbles back to her parents' camper.

And what if there were no one pursuing? No storm
to blow my windows out? I could sleep without whispers,
wake without guarding my eyes.
My friend the rational sunshine
says you're wishful thinking, Santa-Claus daddy
come down through ashes just to indulge me.
Oh, but it's cold on the roof of my life
under the flashbulb moon,
with no rumors of hooves sharpening above.
No one to know when I've been sleeping,
or with whom.

Now that you've gone, I won't look at the shapes of clouds,
dream-beasts that can't resist your tearing apart.
No face remains; love's rubbings even unpaint the doll's cheeks.
Spare me this corner, I said, and you left
the whole field bare
under an endless platter of good weather.
Wishful thinking: that moment darkened by the brush of evening
when the child locked in the toystore wants to be found.

–Jendi Reiter

Marion Wiesel, Wiesel's wife and translator

The Absent Presence in Elie Wiesel's Autoethnographies

Suzanne Evertsen Lundquist
Brigham Young University

A writer cannot detach himself from his story: He is responsible for it to the end. (Wiesel *And* 82)

To date Elie Wiesel has published fifty-nine books—novels, story collections, essays, a play, dialogues, biblical exegeses, cantatas, a children's book, and several autobiographical texts —beginning with *Night* (1960). But Wiesel's literary works constitute only part of his influence. It is his person, his life-experiences as a *Tzaddik*, a Just Man, that drew the Nobel committee to consider him for the Peace Prize. In *All Rivers Run to the Sea: Memoirs* (1995) and *And the Sea Is Never Full: Memoirs, 1969–* (1999), Wiesel contextualizes these experiences that have caused many people to seek his wisdom. These two texts along with the late works of Jewish philosopher Emmanuel Lévinas and Jewish critical theorist Jacques Derrida attempt to name the absent presence that announces the possibility of overcoming injustice—the possibility of a future to come. But identifying the "absent presence" in Weisel's "memoirs" is a task of theoretical complexity involving genre designations (truth claims), questions of ethnic identity, the possibility of a future in an era of terrorism and violence, and the psychological, political, philosophical, and theological difficulties concomitant to surviving the Holocaust.

All Rivers Run to the Sea and *And the Sea Is Never Full* belong to an emerging genre that commences from the perspective of an individual living in pluralistic complexity to address the ethical dilemmas facing human beings in the past hundred years—the age of war. Even though their titles designate them as memoirs, they are, strictly speaking, neither memoir nor autobiography. Students of literary criticism are taught that "[m]emoirs differ from autobiography . . . in that they are usually concerned with personalities and actions other than those of the writer, whereas autobiography stresses the inner and private life of its subject" (Harmon and Holman 305). Wiesel's self-life writings thus seem to be neither of these. Instead, they are literary autoethnographies.

Literary autoethnographies in this context are conscious expressions of how ethnic affiliation, religion, ancestry, gender, life stages, education, profession, geographical locale, and historical moment influence identity. Furthermore, autoethnographies demonstrate that identity is a dynamic process—especially in "times of crisis" (Schick 19). In such texts authors become anthropologists of their own experiences—and those experiences are invariably lived "in relation to collective social units or groupings" (Krupat 212). Authors of such works also attempt to reclaim ethnic identity out of the ashes of oppression, despair, ethnocide, and often genocide.

Autoethnography has a long history, since first contact between Europeans and Native Americans. Mary Louise Pratt defines an autoethnographic work as "a text in which people undertake to describe themselves in ways that engage with representations others have made of them" ("Arts" 585). Wiesel claims that he is answering in his two works the question God posed to Adam: "*Ayekha*, where are you?" For Wiesel, this leads to the "fundamental questions that every human being must confront sooner or later": "Where do you stand in this world? What is your place in history? What have you done with your life?" (*And* 3). In *And the Sea is Never Full*, however, Wiesel moves from descriptions of his "almost reclusive life" as "a young

Talmudist-turned-writer when he returned from the death camps" to a more aggressive stance (4): "I shall take a stand against some of my adversaries, those who have, in my estimation, transgressed the limits of dialogue, having chosen obfuscation as their weapon and 'demonization' as their goal" (6). Pratt calls such a position "the contact zone," a space in which "peoples . . . come into contact with each other and establish ongoing relations, usually involving conditions of coercion, radical inequality, and intractable conflict" (*Imperial* 6). Demonizers in Wiesel's case are more than anti-Semitic outsiders; they are Jewish detractors who publicly contest Wiesel's politics and renown as a means of denigrating Judaism.

In Weisel's case autoethnography is not an attempt to retreat into radical Zionist politics or traditional Judaism or Judeocentrism (*And* 125–30), but, rather, an attempt to use Jewish systems of thought—Midrash, legends, biblical references—to establish peace beyond ethnic particularism and yet be seen from a particular genealogical, historical past. In the words of Derrida, such aspirations turn "on a hope and faith . . . in something radically pluralistic, plurivocal, multi-cultural, heteromorphic, heterological, and heteronomic, something that outstrips what we today call nation and national citizenship" (qtd. in Caputo 174).

Wiesel contends that the years described in his two narratives were "feverish, convulsive" ones that unfolded "under the dual sign of change on a practical level and loyalty on the level of memory" (*And* 5). To the question, "What is the goal of a writer?" he answers, "To testify" (8). Of this goal Garret Hongo says,

> I don't know myself what makes someone feel that kind of need to have a story they've lived through be deposited somewhere, but I can guess. . . . A character, almost a *topoi* [archetype] he occurs so often, is frequently the agonistic who gives personal testimony about an event the rest of his community cannot even imagine. (344)

Certainly, Wiesel was the first to define the deaths of Jews during WWII as a Holocaust—"an offering that has been totally consumed"

(*Messengers* 71)—not that Nazi soldiers were making any kind of spiritual offering, but that the deaths of Jewish men, women, and children can be given meaning by being interpreted as an agonistic sacrifice—a holiness. On the contrary, Wiesel attests, "Precisely because an event seems devoid of meaning, we must give it one. Precisely because the future eludes us, we must create it" (*All* 17).

Wiesel also declares, "I cling to the notion that in the beginning there was the word; and that the word is the story of man; and that man is the story of God" (5). Herein lies the complexity of his ethnographies: if "the word is the story of man; and . . . man is the story of God," both narratives have deeply tragic substrata—especially in the face of the Holocaust and its traumatic aftermath. Alan L. Berger maintains that "[t]he millennial struggle between covenantal claim and historical counterclaim in its twentieth-century expression nearly resulted in the theological and physical destruction of Judaism" (16). For Wiesel, "Auschwitz may well represent a double tragedy, of the believer and his Creator alike. . . . Auschwitz is conceivable neither with God nor without Him. Perhaps I may someday come to understand man's role in the mystery Auschwitz represents, but never God's" (*All* 84).

Despite such spiritual anguish Wiesel still believes in the possibility of justice: "In all my lectures on Jewish themes, I emphasize Judaism's ethics, which, by definition, decry racism. A Jew must not be racist; Jews are committed to fighting any system that sees in the other an inferior being" (*And* 146). When Wiesel won the Nobel Peace Prize, Egil Aarvik introduced him as "a messenger to mankind" whose message is not one of "hate and revenge, but . . . of brotherhood and atonement. . . . In him we see a man who has gone from utter humiliation to become one of our most important spiritual leaders and guides" (4). And yet, Wiesel asks,

> Does this mean that I have made peace with God? I continue to protest His apparent indifference to the injustices that savage His creation. And the Messiah? He should have arrived earlier, much earlier. Perhaps Kafka was right: The Redeemer will come not on the last day but on the day after. (70)

Wiesel's dreams are full of anguish and loss. For example, in one dream he looks "for a familiar face," but "[a]ll the faces are veiled, lifeless. I am panic-stricken," he explains (5). In another, he sees ghosts emerge from shelters and "urges" that he and his father follow them into a "brightly lit synagogue." Once they are in the light, a stranger snuffs the candles, and they are thrust into darkness. Wiesel asks, "'Father . . . where are you?'" Wiesel can "no longer" see his father's face. "Yet, while I still know who he is," writes Wiesel, "I no longer know who I am" (87). Simone Weil explains the nature of such a condition:

> Affliction makes God appear to be absent for a time, more absent than a dead man, more absent than light in the utter darkness of a cell. A kind of horror submerges the whole soul. During this absence there is nothing to love. What is terrible is that if, in this darkness where there is nothing to love, the soul ceases to love, God's absence becomes final. The soul has to go on loving in the emptiness, or at least to go on wanting to love, though it may only be with an infinitesimal part of itself. (70)

In Weisel's case this wanting to love generates his capacity to survive in the face of abhorrent memories.

Such survival, however, must necessarily involve others—especially as it speaks to the notions of futurity, intimacy, and the unacknowledged power of the feminine. In the documentary *Derrida*, Amy Ziering Kofman interviews the philosopher. At one point she asks him, "If you were to watch a documentary about a philosopher—Heidegger, Kant, or Hegel—what would you like to see in it?" In partial jest Derrida answers, "Their sex lives. If you want a quick answer. I would like to hear them speak about their sexual lives." "Why?" Kofman inquires, to which Derrida retorts,

> You don't want the quick answer; you want a justification of the answer. Because it's something they don't talk about. . . . Why do these philosophers present themselves asexually in their work? Why have they erased their private life from their work?

Or never talked about anything personal. There is nothing more important in their private life than love.

Wiesel does speak of his private life—grandparents, parents, siblings, and friends. Yet his two autoethnographies contain few references to his wife, Marion Rose Wiesel. This assertion does not in any way imply that Wiesel is a stereotypical Jewish patriarch who views women as inferior or subservient and, therefore, not worth writing about. In *All Rivers Run to the Sea* he speaks of his childhood in Sighet, Romania. He writes fondly and often about his grandmothers, mother, and sisters—especially Tsiporah, his youngest sister. Of his Grandmother Nissel, for example, he asserts,

> If Grandma had a grave, I would go to the ends of the earth to visit it. But as you know, she doesn't. Did you know she expected that? Did you know, Grandpa, that Grandma Nissel was the only one in the family, almost the only one in the whole community who guessed it all? (9)

Of his mother he says, "Smile all you want, Dr. Freud, but I was attached to my mother, maybe too attached. When she left me to help out at the store, I would tremble under my blanket. When she was away, however briefly, I felt rejected, exiled, imperiled" (10). When Sarah, Wiesel's mother, is told by Rabbi Israel of Wizhnitz, that her son will become a "'*gadol b'Israel*, a great man in Israel, but neither you nor I will live to see the day,'" she weeps with both joy and sadness. "My mother was my sole ally and support," says Wiesel, because "[s]he alone understood me" (13). Of Tsiporah, Wiesel recalls, "There were times when I quarreled with my older sisters, but never with her. We all loved her madly." Everyone in the family spoiled her. "Perhaps we sensed that time was short, that we had to shower her with all the love and all the joys and favors of which she would soon be deprived" (15). Tsiporah's death became a symbol for Wiesel of the suffering of innocence—a keen and personal witness to the unparalleled loss of the 1.5 million Jewish children who were murdered during the Holocaust.

Derrida's insistence that the love life of philosophers is central to the formation of their ideas is a radical position—one that challenges the objectivity of philosophical thought. It also suggests that thought is gendered and that intimacy between a man and a woman, when taken into the consciousness of authors, will force them to reconfigure their thinking. In this context Wiesel's limited references to his wife throughout his life-writings are telling. He speaks of being fearful of marriage because he feared "losing" his "freedom," asking, "Why did I wait so long to create a home? True, I worried about not being able to support a family, but was there a deeper reason, a general lack of confidence in the future?" (*And* 12). Earlier, he recounts,

> In the first volume of my memoirs, I tried to describe the secret, almost reclusive life of a young Talmudist-turned-writer when he returned from the death camps. My peaceful childhood, my turbulent adolescence, the uncertainties of my formative years. Full stops and shaky beginnings. . . . Years marked by messianic dreams and challenges, ecstasy and mourning, separations and reunions. A little girl with golden hair, a wise and loving mother. An ailing and defenseless father. Moshe the Madman, Kalman the Kabbalist. Shushani and his mysteries. Saul Lieberman. . . . Sighet, Auschwitz, Paris, New York: each place a world unto itself. My journal ended on April 2, 1969, in Jerusalem when my life took another turn, this time toward hope. Toward Marion. I got married. (4)

This "turn" towards "hope" is orchestrated by his marriage. His claim justifies readers in expecting a fuller discussion of such a dramatic life change, yet, following the claim, references to Marion are brief.

Wiesel does acknowledge Marion's presence during various post-1969 episodes in his life, but she is often merely a figure in different settings. He spends a few pages describing their courtship—but only a few. In several instances he admits to Marion's influence in his life. For example, he notes, "The failure of my father and of all he symbolized long made me fear having a child. I was convinced that a cruel and indifferent world did not deserve our children." It was Marion who "persuaded me otherwise," he says. Marion advised, "It was wrong to give the killers one more victory. The long line from which I sprang must not end with me. . . . She was right," he confesses (43).

A discussion of the sacred marriage rite—partially narrated in the Song of Songs—is central to an understanding of the "absence" or "lack" in Wiesel's personal narratives. Harold Fisch calls Song of Solomon the "Allegorical Imperative" of which the witness is "espousal" and "gives us access to the mystery of divine love because it is itself an incarnate mystery, a testimony to a transforming encounter, a means of transcending the merely natural" (102); Rabbi Akiba calls the Song of Songs the "holy of Holies" (qtd. in Francis 13); and Phyllis Trible contends that Song of Songs—the sacred marriage—can redeem creation and individuals from apocalyptic events (74). The Song is a lyric testimony to the belief that "love is strong as death" (8:6). Lévinas explains in *Totality and Infinity* (1969) how such redemption is possible.[1] In the chapter entitled "Phenomenology of Eros" Lévinas dances with the idea of the feminine, which he calls *voluptuosity*. This love of the Other, a woman, "is not reducible to the repetition of this *non* [closed, non-public, society], but to positive traits by which the future and what *is not yet* (and is not simply an existent that remains at the status of the possible) is, so to speak, determined" (265). He explains further that "love seeks what does not have the structure of an existent, the infinitely future, what is to be engendered," contending that "[i]f to love is to love the love the Beloved bears me, to love is also to love oneself in love, and thus to return to oneself" (266). Such love also engenders a relationship with the future or "fecundity." In the chapter on "Fecundity" he explains that

> [t]ranscendence, the for the Other, the goodness correlative of the face, founds a more profound relation: the goodness of goodness.

---

[1]Wiesel and Lévinas were both students of Mordechai Rosenbaum— Shushani—whom Wiesel terms "a master," "a holy man in disguise, a kabalist wandering the earth to gather 'divine sparks,'" and a man whose "words banished distance and obstacles." It was as if Shushani could explain "to the Creator Himself the triumphs and defeats of His creation," notes Wiesel (*All* 124–25).

> Fecundity engendering fecundity accomplishes goodness: above
> and beyond the sacrifice that imposes a gift, the gift of the
> power of giving, the conception of the child. (269)

Moreover, he contends that "the encounter with the Other as feminine is required in order that the future of the child come to pass
from beyond the possible, beyond projects" (267). The verb "engen-
der" can also be read as "in gender"; that is, within the loving relationship established between a man and woman, a "good" future
becomes possible through the birth of a child—a birth that witnesses
to the ongoing power of Creation. For Elie and Marion Wiesel, that
futurity came with the birth of their son, Elisha.

In the chapter, "I and Dependence," Lévinas sets forth the propo-
sition that

> [t]he welcoming of the face is peaceable from the first, for it an-
> swers to the unquenchable Desire for Infinity. . . . This peaceable
> welcome is produced primordially in the gentleness of the femi-
> nine face, in which the separated being can recollect itself, be-
> cause of which it *inhabits*, and in its dwelling accomplishes
> separation. (150–51)

Further on, he suggests that

> in founding the intimacy of the home the idea of infinity pro-
> vokes separation not by some force of opposition and dialectical
> evocation, but by the feminine grace of its radiance. The force
> of opposition and of dialectical evocation would, in integrating
> it into a synthesis, destroy transcendence. (151)

In other words, Lévinas asserts that the face of the woman cannot
be possessed or reduced. This is not the reduction of the other to the
same—the conjoining of bodies into some oblivion of two selves.
Rather, marriage and home are the possibility of the future—of the
child. Such a gift is a grace—the presence of what was conceived of as
being absent. Although Marion Wiesel's voice is seldom heard in
Wiesel's writing, she is the presence of his texts. She translates them

from the French. Her English words over Wiesel's French words are "word-cloth," an image of fabric draped over language—much like sacred clothing over flawed bodies. Her voice embraces his and makes it present in those English translations. She is the absent presence. It is her voice heard in every word like a conduit connecting Wiesel's life stories with the world. "Marion, my wife, my ally, my confidante, it is she," Wiesel admits, "who often prevents me from making mistakes. It is to her that I owe the wisdom that enables me to follow a certain path" (*And* 406). Yet Wiesel is generally silent about exactly how Marion is his "helpmeet," his *ezer kenegdo*, equal to him, the one who helped him overcome his aloneness, nor does he speak of how the sacred marriage rite recreates holiness after the manner discussed by Fisch, Trible, Rabbi Akiba, and Lévinas.

Towards the end of *And the Sea Is Never Full*, Wiesel, having turned seventy, contends,

> The century I have lived through has been more violent and more promising than any other. Mankind has never before proved to be as vulnerable or as generous. Man lives in expectation. Expectation of what? The Jew in me is waiting for Redemption. (404)

Elisha (Wiesel's son) and Steve (his sister Bea's son) accompany Wiesel on a trip back to Sighet, Auschwitz-Birkenau, and Buchenwald. In the midst of Wiesel's memories and mourning—over the deaths of his sister Tsipouka, grandmother Nissel, grandfather Dodye, mother Sarah, father Shlomo, among others—he reflects, "Did I say it out loud to my two companions whom I love with all my soul? Ours is the tree of an old Jewish family whose roots touch those of Rashi and King David. And look: Its branches refuse to wither" (*And* 408).

When he laments the possibility that he will not be able to fulfill the work still to be done—"the secrets to discover" as well as the questions "to be answered"—"the door opens," and he hears from another room, "or is it the other side of night, a sweet voice" that "breaks into [his] daydream: 'Did you call me, Father?'" Wiesel answers, "Yes, my son. I called you" (410). Is this final dialogue an allusion to 1 Samuel 3:4 where the Lord calls Samuel and Samuel answers "Here am I"? Is it also an allusion to the "I AM THAT I AM" in Exodus 3:14, the "I am" that came "down to deliver them out of" Egypt (Ex. 3:8)?

From an analysis of the absent presence in Wiesel's life-writings, the desire comes for another volume to be added to his autoethnographies, one which would answer the question, are not Wiesel's wife and son a presence, a promise of the future, a grace from the God whom Wiesel finds absent?[2] Derrida distinguishes between "the future and '*l'avenir*.'" The future is that which "is predictable, programmed, scheduled, fore-seeable." *L'avenir*, however, "refers to someone who comes whose arrival is totally unexpected. For me," says Derrida, "that is the real future. That which is totally unpredictable" (*Derrida*). Wiesel, Lévinas, Derrida—in their Jewishness—speak of futurity. For Derrida,

> Deconstruction situates itself in the gap between all existing democracies, which are not democratic, and the democracy to come, and this precisely in order to keep alive with prophetic fervor a messianic faith in the unforeseeable and incalculable figure of the Just One, of the democracy, to come. (Qtd. in Caputo 175)

John D. Caputo suggests that

> [i]n this messianic aspiration, the hegemonic rule of the most powerful nations, who dominate the so-called 'United Nations,' would be delimited in a new International, one that is attuned to the gratuitous sufferings that ensue from what Lévinas called the hatred of the other. (174)

All three—Wiesel, Lévinas, Derrida—recognize injustice in the world and desire a peace that is messianic, that is yet to come. The possibility of such peace, of futurity in the gift of the beloved and a child, is yet to be a fully articulated presence. The realization of the feminine is likewise yet to come. Yet the bridegroom, bride, and child might be the promise, the Song of Songs that reclaims the loss of God

[2]This article was completed prior to the publication of Wiesel's *The Time of the Uprooted* (2005).

in Eden and Auschwitz, the answer to the question, "Where are you?" Perhaps this non-patriarchal stance is the absence made present—the forerunner to the messianic.

WORKS CITED

Aarvik, Egil. "The Nobel Presentation Speech." *Elie Wiesel: The Nobel Peace Prize 1986.* New York: Summit Books, 1986. 3–11.

Berger, Alan L. *Crisis and Covenant: The Holocaust in American Jewish Fiction.* Albany: State U of New York P, 1985.

Caputo, John D. *Deconstruction in a Nutshell.* New York: Fordham UP, 1997.

Derrida. Dir. Kirby Dick and Amy Zeiring Kofman. Zeitgeist Films, 2002.

Fisch, Harold. *Poetry with a Purpose.* Bloomington: Indiana UP, 1988.

Francis, Landy. *Paradoxes of Paradise: Identity and Difference in the Song of Songs.* Sheffield: Almond P, 1983.

Harmon, William, and C. Hugh Holman. "Memoir." *A Handbook to Literature.* 9th ed. Upper Saddle River, NJ: Prentice Hall, 2003. 305.

Hongo, Garrett. "Kubota." *American Mosaic: Multicultural Readings in Context.* Ed. Barbara Roche Rico and Sandra Mano. Boston: Houghton Mifflin, 1995. 338–46.

Krupat, Arnold. *Ethnocriticism.* Berkeley: U of California P, 1996.

Lévinas, Emmanuel. *Totality and Infinity: An Essay on Exteriority.* Pittsburgh: Duquesne UP, 1969.

Pratt, Mary Louise. "Arts of the Contact Zone." *Ways of Reading: An Anthology for Writers.* 5th ed. Ed. David Bartholomae and Tony Petrosky. New York: Bedford/St. Martin's P, 1999. 582–600.

———. *Imperial Eyes.* London: Routledge, 1992.

Schick, Irvin Cemil. *The Erotic Margin: Sexuality and Spatiality in Alteritist Discourse.* London: Verso, 1999.

Trible, Phyllis. *God and the Rhetoric of Sexuality.* Philadelphia: Fortress, 1978.

Weil, Simone. *Waiting for God.* 1951. New York: Perennial Classics, 2001.

Wiesel, Elie. *All Rivers Run to the Sea: Memoirs.* Trans. Marion Wiesel. New York: Shocken Books, 1995.

———. *And the Sea Is Never Full: Memoirs, 1969–*. Trans. Marion Wiesel. New York: Alfred A. Knopf, 1999.

———. *Messengers of God.* 1976. Trans. Marion Wiesel. New York: Simon and Schuster, 1985.

———. *Night.* Trans. Stella Rodway. New York: Hill and Wang, 1960.

———. *The Time of the Uprooted.* Trans. David Hapgood. New York: Alfred A. Knopf, 2005.

Itskhok Leybush Pertez (1852–1915)
Postcard, c. 1910
Benjamin Swartzberg Collection, Chicago

Elie Wiesel and I. L. Peretz

Hannah Berliner Fischthal
St. John's University

Despairing of the present, man seeks beauty in legends.
(Wiesel *Souls* 257)

In the first volume of his splendid autobiography, *All Rivers Run to the Sea: Memoirs* (1995), Elie Wiesel mentions without elaboration that Itskhok Leybush Peretz, the recognized father of Yiddish literature, is his "hero" (355). Why Peretz? Wiesel, whose heart and soul have rejoined those of the Hasidim he had so loved in his childhood in Sighet, Romania, and who has already published at least three volumes and given many lectures celebrating the renowned Hasidic masters, is seemingly distant from Peretz, the Socialist who satirized rebbes and their disciples in the hope of enlightening and modernizing a backwards sect. Nevertheless, in a review of Peretz's *Selected Stories* (1974), Wiesel avers he admires and is inspired by Peretz ("Victims" 323). He also endorses a newer *I. L. Peretz Reader* (1990): "If you want to discover the beauty, the depth, the unique wonder of Yiddish literature—read the volume by its Master," Wiesel announces on the back cover.

The backgrounds of the two writers are undeniably different. Wiesel joyfully followed the ways of his beloved grandfather, a Wizsnitzer

Hasid, until they and all the Jews in Hungary were deported to Auschwitz in 1944. In contrast, Peretz, brought up in a traditional Orthodox manner, was taught to shun the Hasidic heretics. He was born and reared in Zamość, a walled fortress town in the Russian Pale (later Poland), a place where Hasidim were, according to Peretz's memoirs, simply "kept out of the city. If Zamość got word that a rebbe was on his way, the police were asked to set a guard at every gate, and the community provided a Jew to stand by him on watch" ("My" 321–22).

In Warsaw, where Peretz relocated after he had been disbarred by the tsarist government with no explanation, he continued to be appalled by the Hasidim for refusing to accept science, for degrading women, and for contributing to the stagnancy and poverty of their *shtetlekh*. He worked for a Jewish agency collecting data about Jews. At the same time in his essays and news columns he "never ceased to criticize the Hasidim for their fundamentalist beliefs and their resistance to change" (Wisse xxi).

A socialist idealist who spent three months in prison for his radical views, Peretz aimed to improve. His popular stories were hailed by many as neo-Hasidic; but the underlying messages of the tales were anti-Hasidic. As David Roskies puts it, subversion lurked "beneath the pious façade" of Peretz's works (7). Maurice Samuel calls Peretz not only Prince of the Ghetto but "a divided man" (121), because he seemed both to love and hate his fellow Jews. Peretz, more subtle than de Maupassant, was a master of the ironic twist. Sympathy unexpectedly gives way to criticism. In "Kabbalists," for example, a penniless yeshiva student starves himself to death, hoping to attain the Kiss of Moses described in the Kabbala. While Peretz portrays the scene with some pity, he makes it clear that the situation is tragic and unnecessary.

Ideologies aside, however, Peretz the artist, who wrote in Hebrew but more often in Yiddish, was largely responsible for introducing the Hasidic tale into modern literature. Like Berdichevsky and other Yiddish writers, Peretz became aware of the treasures of Hasidic literature: wonder tales, allegories, parables, stories of wisdom, revelations of the Torah, mysteries of the Kabbalah. In addition, "Hasidic tales contained a wealth of poetic imagery and lyricism, symbolism and subtlety" (Dawidowicz 68). Hasidism thus infused Yiddish literature, which was somewhat stuck in the preaching Haskala (Enlightenment) mode, with new vigor.

Peretz used his genius to cultivate legends of the Hasidic rebbes and then reshape them according to his humanistic and secular beliefs. As Irving Howe and Eliezer Greenberg put it, Peretz reworked folk and Hasidic tales "in a way that appears to be folklike but is actually the product of a sophisticated literary intellect" (14). He somehow sapped the essence of a story, removed the piety, and rewrote it so that it became a paradigm of clarity, vision, and morality. Ken Frieden states that Peretz's stories had a direct influence on Martin Buber, who became more aware of them around 1901, when Peretz was being honored in Warsaw. Buber began publishing his own neo-Hasidic stories in 1905–06. Says Frieden, "Wiesel is one of the most compelling in a long line of latter-day retellers of Hasidic stories."

Wiesel is one of the greatest aficionados of stories; he even boldly proclaims that "God made man because he loves stories" (*Gates* 10). His devotion to Hasidism is directly linked to what he considers to be "the most important aspect of Hasidism. . . . [I]ts teachings are transmitted . . . in tales—in legends" ("Letter" [14 April 1971] 78). Wiesel praises Peretz, the "admirable storyteller," who "weaves a melodious and evocative spell. His language is at once poetic and down-to-earth, lyrical and interspersed with wit. With one sentence, one image, he succeeds in restoring to us a Jewish world long since vanished, the world of the *shtetl*, with all its poverty and nostalgia" ("Victims" 321).

"If Not Higher" (1900) is perhaps the most famous Hasidic tale that Peretz reframed, giving it, as usual, unforeseen developments. The inner story is a familiar one about Rebbe Moshe-Leib of Sassov (Howe and Greenberg 15). Whereas Wiesel presents other stories about this Rebbe, Peretz adds the Litvak to the popular tale. To Polish Jews like Peretz, Litvaks (Jews from Lithuania) are stereotypically dry, humorless rationalists. They speak a different (and therefore funny) Yiddish dialect and base their lives on the Talmud. Hasidic melodies and dances are forbidden. When Hasidism quickly spread through Eastern Europe in the eighteenth century, Litvak rabbis banned it;

they even excommunicated a few renowned rebbes. Wiesel vividly brings these historical conflicts to life in *Souls on Fire* (1972) and *Four Hasidic Masters and Their Struggles Against Melancholy* (1978).

In Peretz's story, the Litvak, being, of course, a skeptic, decides to find out empirically where the Nemirover Rebbe is spending his days; he does not believe the Hasidim who assert that their holy leader ascends to heaven in order to intercede for his people. The Litvak has the chutzpa to hide under the Rebbe's bed and stalk him as he goes out in the cold early morning. To the Litvak's astonishment, he secretly witnesses the Rebbe changing into peasant's clothing. Then, he sees how the disguised Rebbe chops wood, brings it to a bedridden widow, and lights the fire in her dark, chilled hut. These good deeds affect Peretz's Litvak deeply, turning him into a staunch disciple of the Rebbe: the next time someone murmurs that the Rebbe spends his days in heaven, the converted Litvak quietly answers, "if not higher" (181).

The Hasidic rebbe is heroic not because of his great piety, nor because he performs miracles, fasts and prays all day, and delves into the mysteries of the Zohar, nor because he confers his blessings on everyone around him. To the contrary, he performs concrete good deeds on earth, where they are sorely needed. This is true righteousness. The Litvak's appreciation underlines the message.

Interestingly, Wiesel calls Peretz the "rebbe of Yiddish literature" because, like the Nemirover, he unselfishly aided others. Peretz received, guided, enlightened, and inspired many aspiring young writers. "Like Hasidim coming to their rebbe, they came to him in Warsaw," reports Wiesel ("Victims" 321). In 1915 when Peretz died, a throng of 100,000 Jews converged at his funeral in Warsaw to mourn the gifted writer. His popularity, as well as his literary impact, was apparently colossal.

Peretz's "Bontshe Shvayg," one of his best known tales, deals with an insignificant pauper who, despite bitterly and unjustly suffering all his life, never once complains to people or to God. The story was greatly acclaimed in progressive circles for its argument that the degraded poor need to protest their condition and not meekly wait to ask for a buttered roll from the Heavenly Tribunal. The judge tells Bontshe, "There, in the world below, no one appreciated you. You yourself never knew that had you cried out but once, you could have brought down the walls of Jericho. You never knew what powers lay within you" (151). Bontshe's quiet acceptance of his misery, no matter how saintly it seems, proves needless and meaningless. Peretz blatantly asserts that being quiet is a hindrance to justice and progress. Bontshe "was born in silence. He lived in silence. He died in silence. And he was buried in a silence greater yet" (147). Had Bontshe spoken up for himself as a human being, he would have been able to partake of at least a few of the pleasures of life.

Wiesel singles out "Bontshe Shvayg" for discussion. Bontshe, he writes, is "the meekest among the meek, the eternally offended, the condemned; Bontsha [*sic*] who has never known a moment of respite, of serenity; who has received nothing but blows and insults from life; who has never complained." When offered a reward by the celestial judge, Bontshe cannot imagine what he wants. Wiesel, as usual, asks the astute questions: "But who is to blame? Mankind which has humiliated him too long? God who did not intervene soon enough?" The story, continues Wiesel, is "timeless" and "also reflects the Jewish condition of today: the generation that is mine could have shouted so loud that it would have shaken the world. Instead it whispered, content with its 'buttered roll'" ("Victims" 322–23).

Wiesel actually uses the same Yiddish verb, *shvaygn* (to keep quiet), in his groundbreaking *Un di velt hot geshvign* (1956). In that first autobiography, Wiesel, of course, condemns the silence of the world while six million innocent Jews were tortured and incinerated. He has also criticized Soviet secret police for having used silence "as the most refined of tortures" ("Letter" [15 April 1980] 114). In these instances Wiesel and Peretz are in agreement about the evils of what Wiesel terms "practical silence, which is the mark of the indifferent ones" ("In the Shadow" 111).

In general, however, Wiesel ascribes huge significance and depth to words unspoken. His appreciation of silence, according to Alan Rosen, is partially based on Jewish religious texts.[1] Wiesel reports

---

[1] I am indebted to Alan Rosen for pointing out Jewish religious sources, such as the *Pirkei Avos*, that praise silence.

that "some Hasidim used to boast that they went to the Pshishker. . . 'to listen to the rebbe's silence'" ("Storyteller's" 57). Regarding his own writing, Wiesel believes "in the words you do not say" ("Tales" 60). He admits he is "obsessed with silence because I am afraid of language" and declares that "a work of art can be judged by its weight of silence" ("In the Shadow" 111). He speaks of aiming for "a very eloquent silence, a screaming silence, a shouting silence"; he also speaks of "the power of silence," "silence with a capital S," and silence as a character in his text *The Jews of Silence* (1966) ("Use" 82).

As a matter of principle, Wiesel embraces inconsistencies. Hasidism teaches "that contradictions are an intrinsic part of man," he explains (*Souls* 9). "I'm not against contradictions," he says (Wiesel and Heffner 154). Wiesel's "favorite words" are "and yet" (124). This phrase, occurring throughout his works, also forms the title of the beautiful concluding chapter in the second volume of his memoirs, *And the Sea Is Never Full: Memoirs, 1969–* (1999). Because of his determined willingness to be open and non-judgmental, Wiesel can appreciate a finely crafted tale by Peretz and fully accept (but not necessarily agree with) Peretz's authorial intention.

For Peretz, too, displays inconsistencies which only broaden and enhance his writing. Indeed, Peretz admits in his memoirs to an appreciation of the spiritualism of the very Hasidim he denigrates. He speaks fondly of Reb Mikhl, one of his childhood teachers, who was later rumored to be a covert Kotsker Hasid. "If he was a Kotsker, he would have had to keep it secret; our city was anti-Hasidic, and the study house too," he recollects. Peretz remembers an incident when his town's shrunken innkeeper, "who was so old and frail the merest breath could blow him away," leaped over tables and benches to slap the face of a large stranger who had blurted out words from a prayer about Redemption "that only Hasidim used." Peretz claims he learned nothing scholarly from Reb Mikhl, but he asserts that "if I did no more than copy his silence, I must have absorbed from it the good-hearted sorrow that I recognize in some of my writings. Maybe those meditative eyes passed on to me a little of his Hasidism?" he asks ("My" 273).

Wiesel undoubtedly appreciates the tenderness with which Peretz writes his tales. Peretz may portray his characters as being totally wrong in hanging on to their traditional religious beliefs, but they are victims. Wiesel is most famous for writing about Holocaust victims; of course, the situations are incomparable. However, Wiesel favorably contrasts Peretz's love for his characters with their treatment by a writer like Isaac Bashevis Singer. (Wiesel is too gentle to supply his name, but the reference is obvious):

> Rather than turn them into caricatures, monsters obsessed by sex or money, he shows their human vulnerability, their simplicity; he shows them as victims of society, victims of God, but victims always. Instead of judging them, he takes their defense, fighting the injustices that befall them. ("Victims" 321–22)

Wiesel always values Peretz's "brotherly love for the most wretched" (322).

Similarly, Wiesel lauds Peretz's "social consciousness" because Peretz glorifies the most humble and obscure. Wiesel dismisses Socialism and politics altogether. Peretz's emphasis on the abject, states Wiesel,

> explains why certain scholars stress the importance of social consciousness in Peretz's work. Rightly or wrongly, no matter; let us simply say that his consciousness is essentially Jewish, therefore sensitive to injustice in any form. His response: he loves the poor but not poverty; he admires the humble but he opposes submissiveness. (322)

One of Peretz's *folkstimlekhe* (folk-like) stories, "Three Gifts" is similar to "Bontshe Shvayg" in that it appears to laud Jewish martyrdom while at the same time underlining its tragic purposelessness. A Jewish soul, trying to get through the heavenly gates, attempts to bribe his way in by offering gifts to the saints in paradise. The first present is a handful of "bloody earth," soil from the Holy Land for which a Jew was stabbed to death as he tried to protect it (226). The soul acquires the second gift from a Jewish girl who pinned her skirt to her legs while being dragged to death. She had been sentenced to have her long braid tied to the tail of a wild horse for the crime of "stealing out of the ghetto," looking at the sacred Christian procession, and thus defiling it (227). The gift here is a "bloody needle" pulled from the girl's leg, which retained her modesty. The third offering is a blood-soaked yarmulke. A Jewish victim was forced to run the gauntlet between soldiers wielding knouts. Nobody knew what he had done to deserve this punishment. Halfway through the beatings, his skullcap was knocked off. He "turned around to retrieve the fallen cap" and started back down the line, "soaked in blood but serene" (230). When he collapsed, the soul seized the yarmulke and brought it straight to heaven. The saints, who enjoy getting gifts, admit him immediately to eternity in paradise. A voice up above declares, "Ah, what beautiful gifts! Of course, they're totally useless—but to look at, why, they're perfection itself!" (230).

"Beautiful gifts" indeed. While some pious Jews may appreciate the holiness of martyrdom, of dying *af kidush haShem* (for the holy Name), Peretz punctures and deflates a religious value system in which gory gifts are prized and pain is ignored. The angels acknowledge the torment of the Jewish victims merely by calling it "useless."

Wiesel's first drama, "A Black Canopy, A Black Sky," performed to mark the twenty-fifth anniversary of the Warsaw ghetto uprising, contains a moving scene reminiscent of Peretz's third gift:

> A German hit him with his rifle. The Rov kept right on walking. A second German tore off his hat and threw it into the mud. The Rov bent down to pick up his hat, but the German gave him another blow with his rifle-butt. So the Rov took a handful of mud and smeared it on his head. Then he went on— with his head covered. (23)

There is an innate nobility in both Peretz's and Wiesel's martyrs; they would have suffered less had they not been so concerned with the Orthodox injunction that a man must cover his head. Peretz underscores that all the suffering is "useless." Wiesel might again pointedly ask, as he did of Bontshe's sad life, "but who is to blame?" Wiesel, though he presents his Rov with a dignity that even the murderous Nazis cannot defile, often decries Jewish suffering. This contrasts with the religious point of view which encompasses God's plan and stresses that human beings merely do not and cannot understand the divine design.

Wiesel's writings seem to echo Peretz's in other places as well. Victoria Aarons, for example, remarks that the vivid dramatic scene in which the gentile townspeople attack Gregor, the child playing Judas in Wiesel's novel *The Gates of the Forest* (1966), reminds her of the devils in Peretz's short story "Yom Kippur in Hell."[2] In the Yiddish tale, Peretz depicts the satanic creatures as "dumbstruck, mouths agape, tongues hanging out, faces contorted" (262). In Wiesel's novel, the anti-Semitic audience is comprised of real but no less satanic people: "Projected out of time they were like wax figures, grotesque and idiotic, without destiny or soul, clay creatures, damned in the service of the devil. Their upraised arms hung in the air, their mouths were swollen" (107). Wiesel adapts a scene out of hell to describe a hellish scene in Europe during the Holocaust.

Peretz met a Hasidic rebbe only once in his life (Roskies 15). His skeptical stories champion morality, justice, education, science, and progress. Though not religious, he learned to understand the attraction of Hasidism, especially the way it provided sparks of comfort to downtrodden Jews who were victims of increasingly terrible pogroms and hideous blood-libels, especially from 1881 on. Jewish life was changing, but not for the better; and this had nothing to do with whether Jewish men were wearing *kapotes* or suits.

Peretz the reformer could not have foreseen that Jewish life as he knew it would be exterminated just thirty years after his own death. Wiesel bears witness to atrocities that should make Peretz's celestial judge weep, not laugh, as he did in Bontshe's case. Largely because of the Holocaust, Wiesel understandably portrays his own Hungarian *shtetl* and the *shtetl* in general with sentiment. He refers to the "warm and colorful world of Mendele, Peretz, and Schneour" ("*Shtetl*" 295). "The world of hasidism . . . is the world of my childhood, and perhaps of my innocence lost," Wiesel explains ("Letter" [14 April 1971] 77). In his essay "The World of the Shtetl," he admits that

---

[2]See page 66 in Aarons's article in this volume.

Jews were continuously victims in Europe, even enduring massacres in 1648 of such horrible brutality that, "in Sholem Ash's [*sic*] words, one would lose faith in the humanity of man" (318).[2] Nevertheless, Wiesel remains pointedly fixed in his affections. His love of Yiddish is also somewhat connected to his aching for the pre-Hitler past:

> I love speaking Yiddish. There are songs and lullabies that can be sung only in Yiddish: prayers that only Jewish grandmothers can whisper at dusk, stories whose charm and secrets, sadness and nostalgia, can be conveyed in Yiddish alone. . . . I love Yiddish because it has been with me from the cradle. It was in Yiddish that I spoke my first words and expressed my first fears. It was in Yiddish that I greeted the Shabbat. I did not say "Shabbat shalom" but "a gut Shabess." (330)

"Need I say that I miss it?" he asks rhetorically about his first fifteen years in Sighet. "Must I say aloud what, in many of my writings, I repeat in whispers? The shtetl is my childhood. I remain attached to it and faithful" (319).

Wiesel deliberately chooses to romanticize and sentimentalize his childhood and his early Hasidic life. His own father, after all, was an emancipated Jew. His literary portrayals are closer in tone to Asch's idyllic "*Dos shtetl*" than to Peretz's disparaging depictions of its corruption and sad poverty. "I know that many villages were not as beautiful as I make them and that many people were not as saintly as I make them," Wiesel admits, "but that is the least I can do for them: to give them their purity. Camus once told me, 'One must approach mankind not through its ugly common point but through its most exalting opening'" ("Creative" 286). Like Peretz, then, Wiesel intentionally crafts his material in a way that makes it appear naive while it is actually sophisticated.

Wiesel is not ironic like Peretz, but neither is he simplistic. Wiesel presents tales of the early Hasidic masters, describing the stories and their legendary rebbes "with fervor" (*Souls* 255):

---

[2]Wiesel is referring to Asch's historical novel *Kidush ha-Shem* (1919).

> The Rebbe: confessor, master, guide and above all: father. He
> does not invoke lightning; he is gentle, kind. As the shepherd of
> an ill-starred flock, he defends it against the iniquities of man
> and heaven. Thanks to him, those who have been tried may
> catch their breath and no longer feel forsaken by the God of Is-
> rael and the people of Israel. (209)

And then, dramatically and unexpectedly, he bursts into questioning survivors' sorrow and rage. For example, he elegantly describes the offer of Rebbe Moshe-Leib of Sassov to dance for his friend, since he had no money, but he follows this lovely story with a chilling passage in which he tries to imagine the grandfather he adored, Dodye Feig, a Wizsnitzer Hasid, "in the train that carried him away" (167). And when speaking of the anger of Rebbe Mendl of Kotzk, Wiesel wonders if he could have foreseen a great fire whose "first victims would be Jewish men and women abandoned by God and by all mankind?" (254).

In short, Wiesel and Peretz are not the polar opposites they might initially appear to be. To begin with, both the Hasid and the social-ist are humanists. Wiesel defines Hasidism as "the apotheosis of hu-manism in modern history"; it stresses "the sacredness of man and what makes him human" ("Letter" [14 April 1971] 77). Similar to the Hasidic masters, Peretz and Wiesel each has his own *nign* (tune). According to Byron L. Sherwin, "Like I. L. Peretz, Wiesel searches for the *niggun* [sic], the melody of past times, in order to find the appropriate melody for our times. In Wiesel's writings, the *niggun* [sic] of the past is transmigrated into the present" (120).

In addition, many of the dreams of the Hasid and the socialist are the same. Both seek justice. Wiesel, in speaking of his favorite leg-endary Rebbe, Levi-Yitzkhok of Berditchev, visualizes him "as a power-ful, invincible defender of the weak, a dispenser of mercy ready to risk all and lose all in the pursuit of truth and justice" (*Souls* 90). These words could be used to describe the ideal socialist reformer as well as the Rebbe; Bontshe would certainly have benefited from either one.

Both Peretz and Wiesel espouse means to elevate the poor, the un-fortunate, the insignificant, the hopeless, all the Bontshes of the world. Wiesel praises "Hasidism's concern for the wretched, for the victimized and forgotten Jew" (*Four* 15). Indeed, this important principle runs strongly and deeply throughout the works of both literary masters.

Another theme common to both authors is that of the modern, rational Jew versus the ancient, mystical Hasid. In Peretz's "If Not Higher," a rational Litvak confronts the Rebbe of Nemirov. In Wiesel's drama *Zalmen, or the Madness of God* (1974), communist Alexey speaks to the Rabbi about Jewish "outlandish ritual, its senseless superstitions[;] your past is a burden—a dead weight that stops you from moving forward." The Rabbi, however, articulates feelings about admiring the twilight and befriending "others who like myself are looking for the source and know where it can be found no matter how inaccessible it seems." And when Alexey answers, "I shall break the chain" (71), he is no doubt referring to the metaphoric *di goldene kayt*, the golden chain that links Jewish generations. *Di goldene kayt* (1903) is additionally the name of one of Peretz's dramas, in which a Rabbi desperately attempts to keep the sacred Sabbath from giving way to the profane weekday. Wiesel also retells the true but "sad story indeed" of Zanz and Sadigur, a bitter example of Misnagdim (literally, "opponents") and Hasidim battling each other ("Zanz" 295–96). It is very similar to Peretz's tale, "Between Two Mountains," which pits the Brisker rov against the Bialer rebbe.

Interestingly, Wiesel in 1975 humorously related his own experience in just this sort of controversy with his esteemed mentor and friend, the late Saul Lieberman:

> My teacher now, Saul Lieberman, is a great Talmudist, probably the greatest of the last ten generations. My troubles with him, in the beginning, were due to the fact that he came from Lithuania and was a Misnaged, an opponent of Hasidism, and I come from the Hasidic milieu and love Hasidism. So there was a little antagonism between us in the beginning. Now I think he understands better that not every Hasid is as horrible as he remembers. ("Inner" 236)

Wiesel and Peretz are both extremely talented writers and masters of clear, unembellished prose. Both punctuate their tales with doubts and questions that appeal to the sensibilities of modern readers who are at once attracted to and appalled by the past. Both appreciate and serve beauty and art—in literature and in their ideologies. Wiesel also feels that "Hasidism stresses the element of beauty in Judaism. . . . It teaches us that Judaism is not only religion, not only philosophy, not only ethical principles, but also a work of art: It contains beauty" ("Letter" [14 April 1971] 78).

Wiesel's narrator in *The Testament* (1981) reads Peretz among other free-thinkers and refers to "our great poet Y. L. Peretz" (89, 45). Wiesel himself promises that "to read Peretz is to plunge into an ancient dream and the fervor it calls forth. You will emerge the richer for having done so" ("Victims" 323). The same is true of Peretz's disciple Elie Wiesel: you will emerge far richer for having read his work.

WORKS CITED

Aarons, Victoria. Personal Interview. 27 May 2005.

Asch, Sholem. "*Dos shtetl.*" *Dos shtetl, R. Shlome Nogid, Der farborgener bokher.* New York: Ikuf, 1947. 7–133.

————. *Kidush ha-Shem.* New York: Forward's, 1919. 9–194.

Dawidowicz, Lucy S., ed. *The Golden Tradition: Jewish Life and Thought in Eastern Europe.* New York: Holt, 1967.

Frieden, Ken. E-mail to Hannah Berliner Fischthal. 22 July 2005.

Howe, Irving, and Eliezer Greenberg, eds. *Selected Stories by I. L. Peretz.* New York: Schocken Books, 1974.

————. Introduction. *Selected Stories by I. L. Peretz.* New York: Schocken Books, 1974. 7–19.

Peretz, I. L. "Between Two Mountains." Trans. Goldie Morgentaler. *I. L. Peretz Reader.* Ed. Ruth R. Wisse. New York: Schocken Books, 1990. 184–95.

————. "Bontshe Shvayg." Trans. Hillel Halkin. *I. L. Peretz Reader.* Ed. Ruth R. Wisse. New York: Schocken Books, 1990. 146–53.

————. *Di goldene kayt: a khsidishe familyen drame.* 1903. *Die verk fun Yitshak Leybush Perets.* 13 vols. New York: Farlag, 1920. Vol. 9.

————. "If Not Higher." Trans. Marie Syrkin. *I. L. Peretz Reader.* Ed. Ruth R. Wisse. New York: Schocken Books, 1990. 178–81.

———. "Kabbalists." Trans. Shlomo Katz. *I. L. Peretz Reader*. Ed. Ruth R. Wisse. New York: Schocken Books, 1990. 152–56.

———. "My Memoirs." Trans. Seymour Levitan. *I. L. Peretz Reader*. Ed. Ruth R. Wisse. New York: Schocken Books, 1990. 263–359.

———. "Three Gifts." Trans. Hillel Halkin. *I. L. Peretz Reader*. Ed. Ruth R. Wisse. New York: Schocken Books, 1990. 222–30.

———. "Yom Kippur in Hell." Trans. Hillel Halkin. *I. L. Peretz Reader*. Ed. Ruth R. Wisse. New York: Schocken Books, 1990. 258–62.

Rosen, Alan. Personal interview. 27 May 2005.

Roskies, David. *A Bridge of Longing: The Lost Art of Yiddish Storytelling*. Cambridge: Harvard UP, 1995.

Samuel, Maurice. *Prince of the Ghetto*. New York: Alfred A. Knopf, 1963.

Sherwin, Byron L. "Wiesel's Midrash: The Writings of Elie Wiesel and Their Relationship to Jewish Tradition." *Confronting the Holocaust: The Impact of Elie Wiesel*. Ed. Alvin Rosenfeld and Irving Greenberg. Bloomington: Indiana UP, 1978. 117–32.

Wiesel, Elie. *Against Silence*. 3 vols. Ed. Irving Abrahamson. New York: Holocaust Library, 1985.

———. *All Rivers Run to the Sea: Memoirs*. Trans. Marion Wiesel. New York: Schocken Books, 1995.

———. *And the Sea Is Never Full: Memoirs, 1969–*. Trans. Marion Wiesel. New York: Schocken Books, 1999.

———. "A Black Canopy, A Black Sky." *Against Silence*. Ed. Irving Abrahamson. New York: Holocaust Library, 1985. Vol. 3. 19–28.

———. "The Creative Act: Subject." *Against Silence*. 3 vols. Ed. Irving Abrahamson. New York: Holocaust Library, 1985. Vol. 3. 286–88.

———. *Four Hasidic Masters and their Struggle Against Melancholy*. Notre Dame: U of Notre Dame P, 1978.

———. *The Gates of the Forest*. Trans. Frances Frenaye. New York: Holt, Rinehart, 1966.

———. "In the Shadow of Flames." *Against Silence*. 3 vols. Ed. Irving Abrahamson. New York: Holocaust Library, 1985. Vol. 2. 110–13.

———. "Inner Geography and Outer." *Against Silence*. 3 vols. Ed. Irving Abrahamson. New York: Holocaust Library, 1985. Vol. 3. 234–37.

———. *Jews of Silence*. 1966. New York: Signet, 1970.

———. "Letter to James H. Silberman." 14 April 1971. *Against Silence*. 3

vols. Ed. Irving Abrahamson. New York: Holocaust Library, 1985. Vol. 3. 77–79.

———. "Letter to James H. Silberman." 15 April 1980. *Against Silence.* 3 vols. Ed. Irving Abrahamson. New York: Holocaust Library, 1985. Vol. 3. 114–15.

———. "A Shtetl Grows in Brooklyn." *Against Silence.* 3 vols. Ed. Irving Abrahamson. New York: Holocaust Library, 1985. Vol. 2. 295–96.

———. *Souls on Fire: Portraits and Legends of Hasidic Masters.* Trans. Marion Wiesel. New York: Random House, 1972.

———. "The Storyteller's Prayer." *Against Silence.* 3 vols. Ed. Irving Abrahamson. New York: Holocaust Library, 1985. Vol. 2. 55–59.

———. "Tales Change People." *Against Silence.* 3 vols. Ed. Irving Abrahamson. New York: Holocaust Library, 1985. Vol. 2. 60–61.

———. *The Testament: A Novel.* Trans. Marion Wiesel. New York: Summit Books, 1981.

———. *Un di velt hot geshvign.* Buenos Aires: Tsentral-Farband fun Poylishe Yidn in Argentine, 1956.

———. "The Use of Words and the Weight of Silence." *Against Silence.* 3 vols. Ed. Irving Abrahamson. New York: Holocaust Library, 1985. Vol. 2. 75–84.

———. "Victims of God." *Against Silence.* 3 vols. Ed. Irving Abrahamson. New York: Holocaust Library, 1985. Vol. 2. 321–23.

———. *Wise Men and Their Tales: Portraits of Biblical, Talmudic, and Hasidic Masters.* New York: Schocken Books, 2003.

———. "Zanz and Sadigur." *Wise Men and Their Tales: Portraits of Biblical Talmudic and Hasidic Masters.* New York: Schocken Books, 2003. 295–315.

———. "The World of the Shtetl." *Wise Men and Their Tales: Portraits of Biblical, Talmudic, and Hasidic Masters.* New York: Schocken, 2003. 316–36.

———. *Zalmen, or the Madness of God.* Adapt. Marion Wiesel. Trans. Nathan Edelman. New York: Random House, 1974.

Wiesel, Elie, and Richard D. Heffner. *Conversations with Elie Wiesel.* Ed. Thomas J. Vinciguerra. New York: Schocken Books, 2001.

Wisse, Ruth R., ed. *I. L. Peretz Reader.* New York: Schocken Books, 1990.

———. Introduction. *I. L. Peretz Reader.* New York: Schocken Books, 1990. xiii–xxx.

Jesus' Final Oration at The Last Supper

You interpret my clenched jaw
into geometry,
an angle leaned into stars, a law
for accidents. Not me.
Truth is, you know me less
than you know the sea, coral-hearted,
strung with weed and nets, fish
blossoming, caught, gutted,
salt drying in your fingernails.
That's the truth, confess.
But I am vaguer than your sails.
I am off course,
broken-compassed, adrift
on cures and indiscretion.
Turn right, I'm there, turn left,
still there, an obsession,
like trying to strap a harness to
a cloud. So just believe
in me as you believe in paintings,
oiled cloth, fraying weave,
poses tightening
around a table like this one,
corners chipped, backlit
as though it were a question.
Then interpret,
survey the scene, its damage
and its joy. Observe what's lost
in perspective: the rage
staining my lips, the blast
of ocean hitting land, the moon
still vivid in blue sky,
floating stone
resonant with the cry

of doves and anxious lambs,
wine dripping on the bottle's neck,
that line of ants who lift some crumbs,
trudge to their hole, come back.

–Michael Hicks

Interior of Wiesel's faculty office, Boston University

More Than a Mentor:
Elie Wiesel at Boston University

Martha Liptzin Hauptman
Boston University

Those having torches will pass them on to others.

(Plato para. 222)

Elie Wiesel is known throughout the world as an author, moral philosopher, and humanitarian activist. Through his efforts and his advocacy for victimized groups, this Nobel Peace Prize laureate has influenced many world leaders, if not the course of world history. Perhaps less famously, since 1976 he has been the Andrew W. Mellon Professor in the Humanities at Boston University. As a teacher, he has touched the lives of thousands of students, who, profoundly changed, have gone into the world bearing his message of peace and hope.

I came to study with Professor Wiesel in September 1976 when he began teaching at Boston University. I had read *Night* (1960), *Dawn* (1961), and *The Accident* (1962), his first three books, and like so many of his readers, I had been deeply moved. Having studied religion and philosophy at Columbia University, I was interested in hearing what this philosophical writer could teach me. At that time I was considering continuing my graduate work. During the fall semester he taught a Holocaust course; it was to be the only class with this particular focus that he would offer at Boston University. He said that it was "too difficult to teach this material." He offered it when no one else was teaching such classes, but now he would leave it to others, often warning them that the subject matter might take its toll on them.

That course ended in December, and in January 1977 I left behind the pursuit of an advanced degree to begin working as his assistant. What I have to share is a very personal view of the man and the students who came in and out of his office and mine during my twenty-seven years of working for him. What I have seen has been a privilege, and it has been deeply rewarding to work alongside a man who has taught me many valuable lessons, most importantly, that one must keep going; no matter what, one must never give up on human beings. For he himself keeps going with grace and humility. There are times when I do not know how he can go on speaking out on behalf of humanity. The world lurches endlessly from one tragedy to another. But he does not stop shouting. Perhaps his model is that of the Just Man found in one of his finest stories, related in *One Generation After* (1970), and also used as a preamble to *The Testament* (1981):

> One of the Just Men came to Sodom, determined to save its inhabitants from sin and punishment. Night and day he walked the streets and markets preaching against greed and theft, falsehood and indifference. In the beginning, people listened and smiled ironically. Then they stopped listening; he no longer even amused them. The killers went on killing, the wise kept silent, as if there were no Just Man in their midst.
>
> One day a child, moved by compassion for the unfortunate preacher, approached him with these words: "Poor stranger. You shout, you expend yourself body and soul; don't you see that it is hopeless?"
>
> "Yes, I see," answered the Just Man.
>
> "Then why do you go on?"
>
> "I'll tell you why. In the beginning, I thought I could change man. Today, I know I cannot. If I still shout today, if I still scream, it is to prevent man from ultimately changing me." (*One* 72)

For Wiesel the memory of his past suffering, the cauldron of the Auschwitz experience, will not let him rest. He flies from New York to the four corners of the world, to teach audiences that we are capable of rising above doing violence to one another, that we can do good. Invitations pour in from around the globe, particularly from troubled communities in Northern Ireland, South Africa, and Eastern Europe, and from college campuses suffering from racism in all parts of the world. He has lived through one of the worst chapters in human history, yet still he believes in the possibility of goodness. So on whom else can these troubled souls call who will not only teach but also inspire? Who else will defuse an explosive situation? Who else will answer the call? Memory makes him respond.

When ceremonies marking fifty years since the liberation of Auschwitz were being planned in Poland for January 1995, and it looked as if the Jewish component would be left out or at least slighted, who else besides Wiesel could with gentle and polite but forceful urging change the course of the entire commemoration? Lech Walesa adjusted his speech; the Poles restructured their ceremonies. Wiesel single-handedly softened what could have been a very difficult and potentially ugly situation.

What can I write here that the informed reader does not already know? Perhaps it relates to my witnessing over all these years the stunning metamorphosis of young people who have been exposed to a master teacher, eminent humanitarian, and humane soul who deeply believes in them and their impact on the future, a man who encourages them to believe in themselves and each other, for in my time with him I observed his impact on the lives of many students, first and foremost as their mentor.

What is a mentor? A teacher. A role model. An inspiration. And Elie Wiesel? Isn't he all of these? Yes, but he is more. Why do I say that? And what do I mean by "more than a mentor"? He has changed the course of many young people's lives dramatically, not only by what he taught them in his classroom but also in personal encounters. I have seen them enter his office for the briefest of appointments, perhaps only ten minutes, and then emerge overcome by emotion. Some wear a look of wonder, some come out in tears, some with smiles.

What goes on in those sessions? Students tell me that Wiesel fixes his gaze upon them, and the ensuing experience is profound. For a few moments the world seems to stop. Often, a meeting with him can be an epiphany for young students. They enter in awe of a renowned personality, but what they then experience are his concern, his genuine interest in them, and his humanity. They realize that he cares about them. As one student said,

> The greatest trait that I value in professors is their ability to talk
> *with* their students, rather than *to* the students. Professor Wiesel
> undoubtedly has better things to do, rather than meet with a
> bunch of college kids for an hour or so every week. But he does
> anyway because he has an obvious love for teaching.

Over and over again, his students have echoed this sentiment, relating to me a sense of true appreciation and gratitude for his time, for his listening to what they have to say when, surely, or so they believe, he has more important things to do. But they quickly learn that for him there is nothing more important than they are. For his students he is a role model like no other they have met, for he is in the world, teaching them not just to do as he *says* but also to do as he *does*, that is, to help make the world a better place.

One sees that "better place" in microcosm in his classroom. As one student related,

> There is not a second of rudeness in his class [which she pointed
> out was not the case in her other classes]. . . . He set the tone. . . .
> [I]t was the most civil class in my life. . . . [M]oreover, out of re-
> spect and love of Elie Wiesel, students are always well-prepared
> and respectful of each other.

Sheila, a music teacher on sabbatical leave from her junior high school and a student in Wiesel's course, "The Philosophy and Literature of Friendship," observed that the teacher/student relationship was a metaphor for "ideal friendship": "in the Ideal, love brings you together, respect pulls you apart, not in a negative sort of way, but you must not overstep your bounds. If it's right, there's always a tension, like a beautiful note played on a string." This "ideal" is what she experienced in his classroom. She described him as "the image of the most gracious scholar who brings the past, the future, and the present together. He is bridging generations." She believes that "Wiesel is the epitome of what a teacher should be: he cares for your intellect; he wants you to stretch, to see things in new lights." After twenty-five years as a teacher herself, Sheila said that for her own soul, taking his class was the most important thing she could have done; she needed to experience his passion; she wanted to bring that passion to *her* students: "How many times are we treated to the presence of a truly holy person?" As for an individual appointment with Wiesel, she reported, "When I went into his office, he was fixing a part of me that I didn't know was broken; he knew more than I did about myself."

A mentor generally leads one step by step, showing the way by holding one's hand. When students ask what they can do to make a difference in the world, Wiesel will rarely give them precise instructions, telling them more often to do something, *anything*, to start somewhere, *anywhere*. And they do. They volunteer to teach English to Russian immigrants; they participate in the "Walk against Hunger," raising money to feed the poor; they organize projects on behalf of Bosnia relief; they work to improve Christian-Jewish relations; they work for human rights; they become Peace Corps volunteers; they go to Israel to work on a kibbutz; they participate in social action at Boston University or in their churches or synagogues; they enter graduate programs in the social sciences or professional schools of law and medicine; they become teachers. But these worthwhile endeavors aside, most importantly, they become better human beings: people who care about a hungry child, a destitute mother, or a faltering father. They learn to care about the dignity of their fellow human beings. Even a student going into the world of business goes with a different sensitivity for his fellow human being than one who did not study with Wiesel.

Students say that his classes are like nothing else they have experienced in all their years at university. His courses have subtitles such as

"The Literature of Persecution," "Suicide and Literature," "Franz Kafka's Exile and Memory," "Fear and Melancholy in Hasidism," "Exile and Redemption," "Biblical Attitudes Toward Suffering," "Literature of Castastrophe," "The Power of the Story," and "The Inner Journey: To Despair or Madness and Back." But all share the same general title: "Literature of Memory." Students read Job, Ecclesiastes, and other biblical selections; they read Camus, Kafka, Goethe, Euripides, Shakespeare, Plato, Nietzsche, Rabbi Nachman, Sylvia Plath, Mary Shelley, Cynthia Ozick, Tolstoy, and Dostoevsky. They study Jewish sources and Islamic poetry. These reading lists draw on the breadth of their teacher's knowledge and interests, spanning biblical, classical, and modern times. No political messages or exhortations are given, yet they are heard again and again in the injunction never to turn away from a hungry child, from a lonely man, from a weeping mother. Students are taught that violence is not the answer.

Most of all, they have the opportunity to study with a man who is himself engaged in effecting change, an individual who is living proof that *one man can make a difference*. His students know that Wiesel is a player on the world stage. When he comes on the scene, others stop and listen. When he speaks, they are moved by his eloquence. Always quiet, gentle, exquisitely well-manned, often poetic, he delivers a message that can bring his listener to tears, to laughter, to action—always on behalf of humanity, never against it. Sometimes, after one of his large lectures (to an audience of hundreds, if not more, of rapt listeners), I have felt that each one there could rise and move mountains. And certainly they believe that *he* can. As he wrote in his Nobel acceptance speech in 1986,

> There is so much injustice and suffering crying out for our attention: victims of hunger, of racism and political persecution. . . . Human rights are being violated on every continent. More people are oppressed than free. How can one not be sensitive to their plight? Human suffering anywhere concerns men and women everywhere. (17)

In the same speech he said, "Wherever men or women are persecuted because of their race, religion, or political views, that place must—at that moment—become the center of the universe" (16). He inspires his students to action. Beyond the given subject matter in a particular semester, he makes them feel not only that they can make a difference, but also that they *must*.

When his students finish a course with him, they understand that they are as important to their professor as he is to them, that he seeks their advice and wants to learn from them as much as they from him. He has taught them to respect each other, to listen carefully to one another, to treat each other kindly. They in turn have become more sensitive to each other's traditions. Their professor, coming from the talmudic tradition, values their questions, stating frequently that while there are not always answers, questions are what count.

Clearly, Wiesel's impact on his students is deep and permanent. Who are they? Where do they come from? Why do they come? With what do they leave? Jew and Gentile, Hindu and Muslim, Buddhist and Mormon, they come from the Far East, North and South America, the Middle East, Europe, South Africa, India, and Pakistan. They come from as many states in America as are represented at Boston University. They are studying the physical and natural sciences, psychology, history, religion, philosophy, English, political science, business administration, theology, communications, creative writing, French literature, and anthropology. They dream of becoming musicians, actors, engineers, artists, doctors, lawyers, businessmen and -women, social workers, ministers, rabbis, and, of course, teachers. Some sign up for his courses simply because they have heard he is a "celebrity," or perhaps they have seen him on television or read his name in the newspaper.

For by far, Wiesel is the most renowned member of Boston University's faculty today. Some students have read his books; some come because their parents have told them that they must take a course with Wiesel before they graduate, some because a parent or grandparent is a Holocaust survivor and their children or grandchildren have heard stories of the camps. For others the opposite is the case: survivor relatives will not speak of Auschwitz, and students believe that Wiesel will answer their questions and unlock the mystery that has burdened them since early childhood.

Regardless of their reasons for enrolling, when the door opens at the first class meeting, a hush comes over the classroom. Some students are awestruck in the beginning, but Wiesel swiftly puts them at ease, making perfectly clear that he is not an icon but very human. He is funny; he smiles; he tells a joke here and there; and he clearly loves to tell a good story. Sneeze, and one will get a "God bless you" from him. His warmth and humility spread over the classroom.

Some years ago when he was to turn sixty, I contacted as many of his former students as I could find, asking them to contribute to a volume of letters as a gift for him. Their responses revealed a loving memory of a teacher who had given them much during their formative years as undergraduate and graduate students. They sent photos of their wives or husbands and their children. They wrote moving tributes. I asked a few of them for permission to share their responses here.

Janet Schenk McCord wrote,

> The bond that forms between any teacher and student is a special one. The tension established is a reciprocal one; it grows and changes as the needs grow and change; but always, once established, the bond holds. Tangible, yet not, it results ultimately in the education of both teacher and student. You challenge me always to look more carefully and critically at the world, to raise the questions, to seek out the meanings, to draw the meanings together and analyze them. To collect the injustices, to call them by name, even when doing so is painful. As my teacher you are a guide, a comfort, a prod, and always you are there as support. And through it all you manage to make me feel as though I have done it all on my own.

When Janet was a doctoral student in the University Professors Program, she was Wiesel's teaching fellow. Dr. McCord is now a member of the faculty at Marian College in Fond du Lac, Wisconsin, teaching Wiesel's work.

Sister Marygrace Peters said,

> "Auschwitzean" anger does not possess him. Neither forgotten nor neglected, the torment and tears forge their way into a world that must remember the life to which it has been called.
>
> New generations are challenged to immerse themselves into what seems to be a sea of inexhaustible suffering, one to which literary genius attests, and submerged there, they are urged to uncover the meaning of hope.
>
> Bloodless neutrality is inconceivable. Instead, the distressing inward cry is transformed, the artificial borders are shattered by words, words that are read and written and spoken ever so gently. Tumors invasive to the human spirit implode and the residue is excised within the discourse of the sacred space that is his classroom.

David Lubars remarked,

> Here was a man who had been honored by presidents, who was internationally known for his uncompromising moral stances, who had written some of the most important books and papers of the 20th century.
>
> But I think we loved him because he never acted like he did.

In later years, David's father, Walter Lubars, a retired professor and former dean of Boston University's College of Communications, has become one of Wiesel's perennial students, saying that after he took his first course with Wiesel, he became "addicted" and now in his retirement looks forward to being enrolled in course after course.

Joseph Kanofsky wrote,

> Elie Wiesel's classes are always conducted on two levels. They concentrate not only on the meaning of the text at hand, but also emphasize its lesson for humankind. The passionate intellect Professor Wiesel conveys kindles a flame of the same nature in his students. Previous illusions are dissected, prejudices exposed,

and attitudes reshaped. One cannot participate in Elie Wiesel's class and not be profoundly changed.

And yet—this is often the case when one studies with great men.

Joseph, having followed Janet McCord as Wiesel's teaching fellow, earned a Ph.D. and is now a rabbi.

Another rabbi, Barry Blum, observed,

> To study with [Professor] Wiesel is an adventure into the depths of melancholy and despair while at the same time appreciating the rich legacy of Judaism which has survived throughout the centuries. He testified to the great evils of humanity, yet is able to express the profound hope in human survival.

Barbara Helfgott-Hyett, now a poet, stated,

> My story is simply one of many. Elie Wiesel is a teacher of such stature, modesty, and grace that only the Bible provides his proper likeness. Not a single one of his students is unchanged; our lives wrapped inextricably in his, and by his, all of us moving outward toward something we can only begin to comprehend. Each of us yearns to be, for him, a kind of David whose voice, our teacher tells us, "alone can dispense the darkness in Saul."

Susan Dodd, a novelist, commented,

> I am indebted to Elie Wiesel beyond expressing. I wanted to be a writer from childhood. Yet it was not until I was blessed by this wonderful teacher's influence, example, and encouragement that . . . I found the courage and hope to try.

Riki Lippitz, a cantor, noted,

> I came to you as a student, but I left you as a teacher. This is, perhaps, the most precious gift you could have shared. . . . If I

have a wish, it is that my children will know what it is to learn at your feet. May they learn your gentleness, your stubbornness and your wisdom.

Patty McAndrews responded,

> My debt to you is great. I learned that questions are important and that due to their very nature need to be asked. A question unasked is like a story untold. I learned that answers are neither quick nor easy and often do not come in a recognizable form. Perhaps the greatest learning was a reaffirmation of something I knew before. . . . If we truly see others as human beings and not as objects somehow disconnected from ourselves then injustice, inhumanity and genocides are far less likely to happen. If I am connected to you then I cannot hurt you without hurting myself. If you cry, then I taste salt. We are completely interdependent.

Surely the torch has been passed to Patty, who after becoming a campus minister spread her teacher's message at a Catholic college. A nun sent a letter which included these remarks:

> Of course, you always remain in my thoughts and prayers, but as the events of the terrible 50th anniversary (the liberation of Auschwitz) came and went and the news coverage featured you so prominently, the memories of those marvelous days of privilege for me in your classroom flooded my mind. . . . This is just to let you know once more how sacred the experience was for me, and how appreciative I am. The example you set continues to inspire me to strive for excellence in teaching.

These words came from Stanley Jacobs:

> Before taking Professor Wiesel's class, I felt indifferent toward Judaism. I was a Jew, and I was content neither to understand nor investigate what it meant to be a Jew. Professor Wiesel shook me from my complacency and left me feeling uneasy with

this decision. . . . [He] made me realize that I was part of a three-thousand-year-old tradition that had witnessed an incredible history: sadness and joy, beauty and ugliness, triumph and tragedy. As a part of this tradition I not only have a responsibility to my past, but to my future; I have the responsibility to bear witness to my people, a responsibility which I share with Moses, Rabbi Akiba, and Professor Wiesel.

One student finds his identity as a Jew and learns about the importance of becoming a witness, of carrying on where Wiesel leaves off. This example may be multiplied by many others over the years who in coming to study with Wiesel take away more than they imagined. They come to learn; not only do they acquire knowledge, but they also find a part of themselves—Jewish or not.

One also sees spiritual growth in students other than those who find a deeper and specifically *Jewish* identity. A Hawaiian student, Kalama, said,

Professor Wiesel, a leader in the Jewish community and one with a firm grounding in the Jewish tradition, stands true to his beliefs without offending students of other backgrounds . . . the unshakable belief he has in his religion couples a great respect for other religions. In this sense, he serves as a model for his students: he encourages them to seek out who *they* are, *spiritually*, while respecting the differences in religion and spirituality of others.

Kalama took another point from his lessons with Wiesel which he transmitted eloquently to me:

One of the reasons I hold a profound respect for Professor Wiesel is because he, unlike many others, was able to take the personal tragedy of his life and use it to help others. Many people allow their experiences to embitter them. After a period of silence, Professor Wiesel confronted his past and successfully tried to understand what happened. He then shared his story with others, and instilled in them hope for a better world as well as the courage to share their own stories. In short, by confronting the past, he overcame the tragedy of his life, and helped others to help themselves.

Finally, Matt, speaking from the Roman Catholic tradition, felt that he had met a "living saint" when he walked into Wiesel's office: "It had the peaceful air of a sacred place, like a cathedral." He felt that by touching the big questions that others would shy away from in a classroom, Wiesel's students are challenged and prepared more realistically for whatever they are going to do in their lives. No one who has studied with Wiesel is given the message that there are simple answers. Matt also was deeply impressed by Wiesel's habit of never being afraid to say, "I don't know." He said, "A friend of mine, who is an admirer and colleague of Professor Wiesel's at Boston University, a professor of philosophy and physics, told me, 'The highest courage is to *bear* living with incomplete knowledge.'" Matt had studied under many professors who were unable to confess that they "didn't know." Wiesel was different. He could, and often did, say that he didn't know the answer, that a question could remain a question.

For his part, Wiesel takes his teaching very seriously. Once, when François Mitterand called him to Paris unexpectedly, he asked me to arrange a telephone hook-up for his seminar so that he could speak to his students during the class hour he would be missing. So from Paris he set the tone for the day, opening discussion on the book they were studying that morning. His students thus learn quickly how much they mean to him. On this day they knew what an effort he had made on their behalf. More often, ironically, they do not know what precedes his getting to his class on a given morning: he could have been flying halfway around the world to make it to his seminar on time. If a snowstorm might prevent him from flying into Boston from New York, then he will take the train.

Let me describe some of the students whose lives have been changed by their encounters with Wiesel. I have mentioned Janet McCord but not her background: heading for a Master of Divinity degree and ordination in a Protestant denomination, she took one class with Wiesel in January 1979 and switched to a Master of Arts program. She decided against ordination and *for* Jewish studies and literature. Only years later did she embark on a path leading to a Ph.D., deciding to study seriously with Wiesel when she returned from Peace Corps service in Africa. As I mentioned, Janet became his devoted teaching assistant, and some seventeen years after her initial encounter with him, she received a Ph.D. in religion and literature. Her dissertation, "A Study of the Suicides of Eight Holocaust Survivor/Writers," was directed by Wiesel.

Fresh from an undergraduate degree in philosophy at the University of California, Santa Cruz, a young Californian with little or no religious background began a journey that led him to a serious appreciation of the Jewish tradition. In the process he became committed not only to religion but also to scholarship and teaching in his own right. Dr. Alan Rosen, also one of Wiesel's teaching fellows, once he had finished his Ph.D. studies, made aliyah. His home has become rich with Jewish song and ritual. A devoted teacher, he has taught in Israel since his arrival there.

A student at Boston University's School of Medicine made the time to take as many courses from Wiesel as she could in order to "humanize her studies in medicine." I believe that she, too, was seeking the richness of Jewish tradition that she found in the hours spent in his classroom. Beth Gordon and her husband Daniel completed their training in medicine after which they lived in Jerusalem for a year, studying Jewish history and philosophy before embarking on their medical careers and rearing their children. They continue to study and learn Jewish texts.

One of Wiesel's students in 1977, coming from India, began immediately to consider herself a disciple, calling herself his "Hindu *hasid*," truly his devoted follower. For five years, Shuma was his teaching assistant. She then became a Unitarian minister. She never stopped regarding him as a teacher who to this day continues to inspire her, even though they are no longer in regular contact.

There was also the pregnant law student who would not miss a class. Her baby was born—as luck would have it—between one class and the next week's session. She brought her newborn son to class, a mere forty hours after giving birth, so she would not miss a day with Wiesel.

There was Reinhold Boschki, a young Catholic theology student from Germany who corresponded with Wiesel for many months. Then, he simply turned up in my office one August day, saying that he had come to study with Wiesel. After reading *Night*, a copy of which a friend had given him, he altered not only his course of study but also his life: he *had* to come and study with Wiesel, and that study became the path on which his life would move from then on. How did his life change? Not only did he become one of Wiesel's devoted students, but he also changed the topic of his dissertation, producing *Der Schrei: Gott und Mensch im Werk von Elie Wiesel* (1994), the first book written on the work and message of Wiesel in German. After the publication of his dissertation, he translated several of Wiesel's books from French into German. Reinhold is committed to spreading the words and teachings of his teacher to both young and old in Germany. In fact, in an effort to combat ignorance and racism and to make a difference in his country, he organized an international conference in 1995, commemorating fifty years since D-Day. His idea was to touch young teachers on this occasion by giving them access to Wiesel's message.

A few more examples of the dedication of this master teacher's students are in order. Carrie traveled on a train two hours each way to study with him. A student at Brown University, she had heard him speak in Birkenau when, as a high school student, she participated in the "March of the Living." Her classmates at Brown could not understand her commitment, but she talked to me of the "aura" Wiesel brought to a classroom that was filled with his presence as well as with reverence and love. She spoke of his gift for creating an atmosphere where everyone felt comfortable. She also spoke of his "incredible passion"—for literature, philosophy, religion, humankind, *life*. His infinite passion was definitely contagious, she said. She felt that he made her feel as if there were nothing a human being, nothing she, could not do: "My generation is a sadly cynical one—Elie Wiesel's passion for life melts the cynicism away."

A student of violin, Julie on leave from Oberlin Conservatory came to Boston University's School of Music for one year. Hearing that Wiesel was on the faculty of the College of Liberal Arts, she enrolled in his Holocaust literature class in the spring of 1982. The following summer, she was a Tanglewood Fellow, studying under some of the world's greatest conductors who came to work with the Boston Symphony and students in residence. Assigned to perform as first violinist in the technically challenging Sixth String Quartet by Béla Bartók, Julie did not realize how emotionally charged this would be for her following her study with Wiesel. Her chamber music coach, Eugene Lehner, was himself a Hungarian who had fled his country in 1939 when anti-Jewish laws went into effect. Lehner has been a member of the Kolisch Quartet, for whom this piece was composed during those turbulent times.

Hearing of Bartók's own escape and knowing of Lehner's, Julie underwent an even more intense professional experience because she had just completed a semester with Wiesel. Through his very being as well as the lessons he taught in that particular class, he had deeply changed Julie. She told me that although she was only twenty-two at the time, she sensed as well as feared that the playing of this Bartók piece might be the musical highlight of her career, and she owed that in part to Wiesel. Bartók's Sixth String Quartet is a farewell to all that was, and in her course that spring Julie had just studied with someone who understood all of that: he had lived "all that was."

The significance of the piece was much greater to her for having read Holocaust literature, which Wiesel has called the "literature of hope." The music includes a farewell filled with profound sadness. A sad slow melody begins each movement, but, interestingly, Bartók concludes the composition with a tiny simple phrase ending on a major chord, which, as in Beethoven's "Ode to Joy" in his Ninth Symphony, leaves one optimistic, if not filled with joyful feelings. Julie's is obviously a story that goes beyond Wiesel's classroom. She said that for her everything converged: literature, history, music, and personalities—Wiesel, Lehner, and Bartók. But her musical experience would never have been as meaningful had she not studied with Wiesel. She shared this story with me thirteen years after it took place, and even then she had tears in her eyes in the retelling.

I return to that phrase, "more than a mentor." What do I really mean? Over the years, unsolicited manuscripts—poetry, essays, and novels—arrived from people unknown to Wiesel, asking for his advice: "Can you help me"; "Is it any good?" Always, an encouraging word was sent in response. Years later, books would arrive with letters from their authors, thanking Wiesel for his support and his belief in them. They said that with his brief words of encouragement, they continued to write, to bring their projects to fruition, to find a publisher. Isn't this being "more than a mentor?" Doesn't this paint a picture of a person who inspires, who by a single word of encouragement, of advice, enables others to do their best? Remember: these people never even met Wiesel, yet something magical somehow occurred. Here is a man who can, just by being who he is and with a simple good word, help aspiring writers to believe in themselves so that work begun can be completed—this is what I mean by "more than a mentor." Whether it is a matter of his own students at the university or unknown and unpublished writers, Wiesel inspires and encourages them all.

Often, young schoolchildren write individual letters in response to *Night*, but more often they write as part of a class because their teacher assigned the book. From eleven to eighteen years old, many seem shaken by this memoir. They identify with the adolescent pain it portrays. Somehow, through his specific and horrific experience, Wiesel gives voice to young people's deepest feelings and fears, unlocking their own stories from the death of a parent to tales of sexual abuse. Those stories are completely unrelated to Wiesel's or, for that matter, to the Holocaust; even so, they need to share them and to relate how *his* traumatic tale has helped them get through *theirs*. I find this striking.

Two examples from high school students must suffice. The first writes, "You are an inspiration to me. I admire you for your success, determination, but mostly for your strength. People like you help bring peace into this scary world. You are a leader and teacher to all." The second attests,

> And now I know that the story of victims who have perished is
> a true story, and how awful it is to be silent when human lives
> are endangered, when human beings are humiliated and suffer.

The most important thing I realized is that it is an offence to persecute people because of their race, religion, or political views. Thank you for your book. It set me thinking about human life and a goal of my own life.

The man who inspired these and so many other responses like them answers every one, signing in his own hand each reply and often inviting the students to come and study with him at Boston University. Some do come, years later, excited by the chance to study with a teacher who has already become their mentor through his written word in *Night*.

In 1973 on the radio broadcast *Eternal Light*, Wiesel commented on his teachers in words that could easily have been uttered by his own students:

If I speak of gratitude, if I feel gratitude, it is certainly because I had teachers who taught me that words are links, that tales are instruments of communication between man and himself, between man and his neighbor, between man and God. God Himself needs words to create, to create man and give meaning to his existence. ("My")

In another broadcast that same year, he said:

To be Jewish is to take a question and turn it into an offering. To be Jewish is to take some fear that is yours and open it up and give it to others, simply to prove that communication is possible, simply to prove that the same fear threatens us all. We are all part of the same generation, Jews and non-Jews. We have the same enemy, face the same menace. To be Jewish is to be human. To be human is to see what others see, to share one's vision with others, to try to break one's solitude, the worst enemy of man today. ("Now")

I believe that in what he offers his students Wiesel is fulfilling the mission he describes in *A Jew Today* (1978), where he says that a Jew's mission is "never to make the world Jewish, but rather to make it more human" (21). We see him in his classroom, surrounded by young people, a master teacher filled with humanity, love, hope, and joy. His students will carry the torch; they will be the bearers of truth and memory.

Works Cited

Bartók, Béla. String Quartet No. 6 in D major.

Beethoven, Ludwig von. Symphony No. 9 in D minor, Op. 125.

Boschki, Reinhold. *Der Schrei: Gott und Mensch im Werk von Elie Wiesel.* Mainz: Mattias-Grünewald, 1994.

McCord, Janet Schenk. "A Study of the Suicides of Eight Holocaust Survivor/Writers." Diss. Boston U., 1995.

Plato. *The Republic.* Trans. [Benjamin Jewett]. *Five Great Dialogues.* New York: Walter J. Black, 1942. 221–495.

Wiesel, Elie. *The Accident.* Trans. Anne Borchardt. New York: Hill and Wang, 1962.

———. *Dawn.* Trans. Frances Frenaye. New York: Hill and Wang, 1961.

———. *A Jew Today.* Trans. Marion Wiesel. New York: Random House, 1978.

———, narr. "My Teachers." *Eternal Light.* Part I. NBC. 1 Apr. 1973.

———. *Night.* Trans. Stella Rodway. New York: Hill and Wang, 1960.

———. "The Nobel Acceptance Speech." *Elie Wiesel: The Nobel Peace Prize 1986.* New York: Summit Books, 1986. 15–18.

———, narr. "Now." *Eternal Light.* Part IV. NBC. 22 Apr. 1973.

———. *One Generation After.* Trans. Lily Edelman and Elie Wiesel. New York: Random House, 1970.

———. *The Testament.* Trans. Marion Wiesel. New York: Summit Books, 1981.

The Anvil of Desire

In the days when wishing was still of some use,
no one had figured out what to wish for.
At the hour when monks threw back their cowls
and drank bowls of soup flavored with one
spongy onion and a lifetime of contrition,
a shimmer emerged from the gorse and grasses
and a cat sat contentedly enclosed in a porch,
marveling not at robins or rabbits on the lawn
but at its own predatory nature. Madmen and
madwomen who were not all that mad looked up
from their after-dinner coffee or whiskey
and thought about warmth and winter and woe.
The sun gathered its fury into itself while
the moon hid in a shadow and apologized
for the darkness. A small feline heart,
forged like everything else in the world on
the anvil of desire, beat without mercy or shame.

–Holly Welker

Book Reviews

Peter J. Schakel, *The Way Into Narnia: A Reader's Guide.* Grand Rapids, MI: William B. Eerdmans, 2005. 202 pp. $14.00

The Way Into Narnia is a reading guide to the Chronicles of Narnia. There are problems with that. One is that only the reading impaired need a reading guide to Narnia; further, even if such a guide were necessary, this one is basic to the point of insult. Reading guides are frank, blue-collar commentary, of course, with few intellectual aspirations and no frenchified pretensions to the rarified air of the higher echelons of literary criticism. But *The Way Into Narnia* depresses that lower-the-level tendency to unprecedented depths.

This guide seems determined to go out of its way to be simplistic, as in the embarrassingly obvious quality of its annotations: "*shoal*: a school of fish" (142); "*cataract*: waterfall" (162); "*duffer*: an incompetent or inefficient person" (152). Definitions such as the last one deftly manage to provide the reader both too much and too little, adding to the insult of pedantry the injury of inaccuracy. Schakel's *duffer* misses what are probably the most pertinent implications of Lewis's term—the wild haplessness, the golf etymology with its windmill flailings, the implications of stiff-jointed agedness. But the fundamental problem with much of the information provided by *The Way Into Narnia* is the way it misses the point in the opposite direction: this reading guide is simplistic, telling readers more about what they already know than they want to be told.

Thus, the bad news is that this guide is sometimes sophomoric. The good news is that Schakel is no sophomore. He stands among a handful of the most recognized C. S. Lewis scholars in the world, one of the very best on Narnia. Additionally, for all the obviousness of his book, it proves ulti- mately a helpful guide, even a valuable one. The value resides almost en- tirely in the book's central insight: Schakel reads the Chronicles of Narnia as myth. His mythic reading, like his annotations, could be deeper, more penetrating, more thorough. But myth is so precisely the essential mode of the Narnia books that Schakel's critical reading, for all its limitations, opens up fruitful avenues into Lewis's literary world. *The Way Into Narnia*, however weak in its details, nails the essence: Lewis's approach to Narnia clearly *is* mythic, so his series is best read as myth.

Schakel reminds readers that Lewis claimed, "'I wrote fairy tales because the fairy tale seemed the ideal Form for the stuff I had to say'" (25). That "'stuff'" in the mature Lewis's fiction is Christian myth. Schakel sees the mythic aspect as the essence of Narnia both in its substance and its incep- tion; he is convinced that the catalyst for that marriage of mythic narrative and Christian image was Lewis's newfound Catholic friend, J. R. R. Tolkien, particularly Tolkien's ideas on *faerie* as set forth in his "On Fairy-stories."

The mythic dimension is as crucial to Lewis as it was to Tolkien and their mutual literary hero, George MacDonald—all three of these titans of Christ- ian fantasy shared the conviction that myth accesses truth. "'What flows into you from the myth,'" according to Lewis, "'is not truth but reality (truth is always *about* something, but reality is that *about which* truth is)'" (35). The juncture of myth and history is thus for Lewis in a kind of practical miracle "Myth Bec[o]me Fact": "'The old myth of the Dying God, *without ceasing to be myth*, comes down from the heaven of legend and imagination to the earth of history'" (350).

That actualizing myth may be what allows Lewis at his best, despite his inveterate allegorizing, to reach beyond allegory—"'into an allegory a man can put only what he already knows; in a myth he puts what he does not yet know and c[oul]d not come to know in any other way'" (36). Echoing that respect for myth, Schakel is appropriately careful in his own tracing of

Christian themes in the Narnia Chronicles to leave implications symbolic, rich emanations of mythic story rather than canned allegorical meanings.

Schakel analyzes those large-scale Christian implications chronologically through the consecutive volumes of the Chronicles themselves. That approach is of course artificial—Lewis's mythic themes, in no way restricted to a single volume, pervade the series. Some themes appear more dramatically or even more widely in books other than the ones where Schakel locates them. But even though the mechanistic analysis makes the thematic implications seem more restricted than they in fact are, Schakel's book-by-book approach has the considerable advantage of clearly demarking major aspects of Lewis's Narnian themes.

The "Christian significance" (44) of Narnia begins to emerge in *The Lion, the Witch, and the Wardrobe* (1950) at the point when Aslan volunteers to stand in for condemned Edmund. Lewis himself called Aslan's sacrifice "'not *allegorical* but *suppositional*'" (44)—his passion and resurrection are the kind of experience Christ might have had in this "supposed" Narnian environment. Lewis, quicker to concede the complexities of atonement than Schakel, struggles with the atonement concept, wrestling it into finite understanding: "'If you think of a debt, there is plenty of point in a person who has some assets paying it on behalf of someone who has not'" (46). And Lewis's Christian myth can work at subtler levels, as when Edmund is redeemed, not simply physically but spiritually, so that, no longer "thinking about himself," Edmund and his life now focus on Aslan.

In *Prince Caspian* (1951) Schakel notes how Narnia characters move from "seeing is believing" to a new faith-based perception: "Believing is seeing" (55). *The Voyage of the Dawn Treader* (1952) is preeminently for Schakel an exploration of the theme of how yearning for the numinous leads to learning. *The Silver Chair* (1953) becomes in Schakel's mythic terms a disquisition on freedom and obedience with a typically Lewisian Christian twist: "Obedience is the road to freedom" (71). *The Horse and His Boy* (1954) examines issues of personal identity from a Christian perspective. *The Magician's Nephew* (1955), in its playing upon endings and beginnings, establishes in the Narnian sphere "something like creation" (94). *The Last Battle* (1956) is most theologically interesting for its "transcendings" (103): in this climactic volume readers encounter most invitingly, particularly after the darkness and death pervading this apocalyptic novel, that Lewisian heaven which is even better than man has a right to hope it will be.

Still, Schakel's mythic analysis, as unfortunately as its annotations, suffers, as previously indicated, from both too little and too much evidence; it manages simultaneously to be both sweeping and pedantic. Yet *The Way Into Narnia*, for all its limitations, establishes persuasively that "the most important effect of the series as a whole is to make room for the spiritual" (117). Lewis's fiction clearly rewards mythic reading. Through the Chronicles of Narnia, itself sometimes as simplistic as its interpretation by Schakel, Lewis achieves some remarkable effects, notably his "recovery of moral law" (117). Lewis's absolute refusal to succumb to modern relativism, his deep mythic allegiance to ultimate values, "achieves in the stories a moral perspective" (117) profoundly meaningful for all Christians. It is a meaning well worth being reminded of, however simplistically.

Steve Walker
Brigham Young University

Davis W. Houck and David E. Dixon, eds. *Rhetoric, Religion, and the Civil Rights Movement, 1954–1965.* Baylor UP, 2006. 1002 pp. $44.95

In *Rhetoric, Religion, and the Civil Rights Movement, 1954–1965*, editors Davis W. Houck and David Dixon have compiled a massive anthology of speeches, prayers, sermons, and funeral orations from the crucial years of the struggle for civil rights. Many of these works have been recovered and transcribed from the Moses Moon Collection, housed at the National Museum of American History in Washington, DC. Other speeches were uncovered through tireless efforts of the editors who combed papers from coast to coast, looking for works to include in this important collection. They ultimately settled on 130 speeches covering over a decade. The judicious selection process and meticulous transcriptions have resulted in a superb document of one of the most turbulent times in American history.

As a work of historical documentation, *Rhetoric, Religion, and the Civil Rights Movement* is a first-rate anthology. Beginning with an "Emancipation

Day Speech" by then Howard University president Mordecai Johnson, delivered a few months before the Supreme Court decision *Brown v. Board of Education, Topeka, Kansas* in 1954, the editors establish the impatient yet hopeful mood of Black America in the days leading up to that landmark court decision that reversed over fifty years of legalized "separate but equal" legislation. Similarly, in a speech delivered the week following the *Brown* decision, Methodist minister Charles P. Bowles urged forward his white Charlotte, North Carolina, congregation with "A Cool Head and a Warm Heart." From optimism and caution in the aftermath of *Brown*, the editors chart a course of growing impatience, frustration, militancy, and indecision that would characterize the next twelve years of the civil rights movement, concluding just after the signing of the Voting Rights Act by President Lyndon B. Johnson in 1965.

On the one hand, many of the speechmakers represented in the volume are among the best known speakers and activists of the time: Roy Wilkins, who served as Executive Secretary of the NAACP, the nation's oldest civil rights organization; Mary McLeod Bethune, inspirational educator and political adviser; Frank Porter Graham, influential liberal president of the University of North Carolina; Adam Clayton Powell, fiery minister and Congressman from Harlem; and youthful John Lewis, former leader of SNCC and one of Martin Luther King, Jr.'s lieutenants, whose impassioned speech at the March on Washington, like most others that day, was overshadowed by King's famous "I Have a Dream" oration. These speeches, typically full of eloquence and fire and charted over the period covered by the anthology, demonstrate a growing insistence on equal rights for all people, as seen perhaps most clearly in Lewis's speech at the Lincoln Memorial on August 28, 1963, which eloquently concludes, "We must say, 'Wake up America, wake up!' for we cannot stop, and we will not and cannot be patient" (587). This insistence becomes even angrier during Dave Dennis's oration at the funeral service for James Chaney in 1964, a speech so emotionally charged that Dennis collapsed in the arms of fellow activist Edwin King and had to be led away to compose himself.

On the other hand, a large number of persons represented in the anthology are not nearly as well known, some even perhaps unknown except to local audiences. These include Lutheran minister and theology professor J. R. Brokhoff, Disciples of Christ minister and Little Rock activist Colbert S.

Cartwright, and NAACP attorney Charles Morgan, Jr. But their speeches are no less impassioned and significant than those offered by more prominent speakers, and indeed their inclusion makes possible a greater appreciation of just how many people across the country were spiritually moved by the cause of civil rights.

Not surprisingly, the editors include very few women speakers in the anthology, owing, of course, to the shadowed positions women often occupied in the civil rights movement. Nevertheless, women are ably represented in the genteel, if naive, address of Sarah Patton Boyle; the inspiring encouragement of the venerable Mary McLeod Bethune; the grief-stricken yet courageous statement of Mamie Till whose son Emmett had been so horribly murdered in Money, Mississippi; and the no-nonsense directness and combativeness of civil rights organizer Ella Baker. Taken together, the contributions of these women reveal a full spectrum of how civil rights activists used the undergirding of Biblical scriptures to appeal to a nation divided over a just cause.

Interestingly, what motivated the editors to seek out these speeches was their admitted ignorance of the fact that religion is crucial to a full understanding of the successes of the civil rights movement. Thus, because they had never heard of the religious traditions in the civil rights movement, they are often a little wide-eyed when they immerse themselves in their discovery. Indeed, just as many audiences, congregations, and other listeners and viewers were spiritually swayed by these speeches, so were the editors, as they continued to uncover and piece together this moving sampling of civil rights rhetoric. Although scripture had long been used to infuse power into the civil rights movement, it had escaped these editors until they became engaged in their project.

If *Rhetoric, Religion, and the Civil Rights Movement* has shortcomings, one would be that the book itself is rather unwieldy. Numbering over a thousand pages, its mere size is somewhat daunting, even to those whose fields of inquiry are well served by the revelations and confirmations it contains. In addition, because many readers are not likely to have the benefit of having heard the delivery of a specific speech, much of what appears in written form falls rather flat. For example, although Dr. King's "I Have A Dream" speech is an excellent model of religious rhetoric at work, part of its real power derives from King's incomparable delivery. His voice reverberates in the ears of those who heard him long after the conclusion of his speech. Because readers will not have a similar frame of reference for the speeches presented in this book, no such enduring quality will be present. Since the editors admit that they were often moved by listening to some speeches, not merely by reading them, that a CD did not accompany the volume is surprising. While the cost of such a CD might have been prohibitive, such ancillary material would nonetheless have made a tremendous contribution to the overall usefulness and appreciation of the book. Even so, one cannot fail to acknowledge the work that went into compiling this anthology. As a project of recovery, it has few peers. Additionally, the editors furnish extensive headnotes to the speeches that provide necessary biographical and historiographical information to offer a rich context for considering them. *Rhetoric, Religion, and the Civil Rights Movement, 1954–1965* is a book that scholars will find most useful, though general readers will likely shy away from such a dense volume.

Warren J. Carson
University of South Carolina Upstate

Blind in Saint Peter's

The blind man comes to see the Vatican. His eyes roll in their sockets over the flight of stairs, still united in their reason for not being. He enters the temple: they float from pope's tomb to pope's tomb, now separated from their useless center, and hear, without reading it, the word *cupola*.

And, uselessly, they don't get lost. Everything is made of invisible substances. The marbles and the columns are too tactile. The gold and the wood advance in vain. And the eyes of the blind man bolt: they touch scrolls and cornices, they slide across the altars, abacuses, cavities, cross-sleeves, arches, and great pommels.

And, finally, they fall at the feet of the gilded glory. Despairing of the answer.

–translated from the Spanish of Ángel Crespo by Steven J. Stewart

Victoria Aarons, professor of English at Trinity University, has written widely on American Jewish literature and culture and on the literature of the Holocaust. Her books, *A Measure of Memory: Storytelling and Identity in American Jewish Fiction* and *What Happened to Abraham: Reinventing the Covenant in American Jewish Fiction*, both received a Choice Award for Outstanding Academic Books.

Alan L. Berger is the Raddock Family Eminent Scholar Chair of Holocaust Studies and directs the Center for the Study of Values and Violence after Auschwitz at Florida Atlantic University. Among his books are *Children of Job: American Second Generation Witnesses to the Holocaust*; *Second Generation Voices: Reflections by Children of Holocaust Survivors and Perpetrators*, co-edited with his wife Naomi, which won the B'nai Zion National Media Award; and *Encyclopedia of Holocaust Literature*, co-edited with David Patterson, which received a Booklist Best Reference Book of 2002 award and was named an Outstanding Reference Source in 2003 by the Reference and User Services Association of the American Library Association. He also guest edited a special issue of *Literature and Belief* on the Holocaust in 1998.

Warren J. Carson, professor of English, is currently Assistant Dean of Arts and Sciences at the University of South Carolina Upstate. A member of the Editorial Board of the *College Language Association Journal* and a reviewer for *Black Issues Book Review*, he has written a number of essays on African American literature and culture. Most recently, he has written a chapter for the forthcoming *Cambridge History of African American Literature*.

Brian Doyle is the editor of *Portland Magazine* at the University of Portland and the author of eight books of essays, nonfiction, and "proems," most recently *Epiphanies & Elegies*.

Ellen S. Fine, professor emerita of French at Kingsborough Community College of the City University of New York, is the author of

Legacy of Night: The Literary Universe of Elie Wiesel, co-editor of the Holocaust issue of *Centerpoint*, and contributor to various books, including *Breaking Crystal: Writing and Memory After Auschwitz, Jewish-American History and Culture: An Encyclopedia*, and *Writing and the Holocaust*. She served as Special Advisor to Elie Wiesel when he was Chairman of the U.S. Holocaust Memorial Council.

Hannah Berliner Fischthal, associate professor of English at St. John's University and co-book review editor of *Studies in American Jewish Literature*, is the daughter of a Holocaust survivor.

Martha Liptzin Hauptman, a graduate of Barnard College and Columbia University in philosophy of religion, was personal assistant to Elie Wiesel for twenty-seven years.

Michael Hicks is a professor of music at Brigham Young University, a composer of experimental chamber music, and the author of *Mormonism and Music, Sixties Rock: Garage, Psychedelic, and Other Satisfactions*, and *Henry Cowell, Bohemian*, as well as many articles about twentieth-century music and Mormon history.

Thomas A. Idinopulos in 1999 founded the Jewish Studies Program at Miami University of Ohio which he directed for seven years and has written ninety articles and thirteen books; his study, *Betrayal of Spirit: Jew-hatred, Holocaust, and Christianity*, is forthcoming.

Suzanne Evertsen Lundquist is an associate professor of English at Brigham Young University and the author of *Trickster: A Transformation Archetype* and *Native American Literatures: An Introduction*. She has also written several articles on Native American and Jewish-American literature.

Julie L. Moore has written a poetry chapbook, *Election Day*. Her poems have appeared or are forthcoming in *Sou'Wester, River Oak Review, Blueline, Sow's Ear Poetry Review*, and *McGuffin*, where her work recently won second honorable mention in the 2006 National Poet Hunt Contest judged by Laurence Lieberman.

David Patterson is the Bornblum Chair in Judaic Studies at the University of Memphis where he is Director of the Bornblum Judaic Studies Program. A winner of the Koret Jewish Book Award, he has published more than a hundred articles and book chapters on philosophy, literature, Judaism, and Holocaust Studies. Among his many books are *Pilgrimage of a Proselyte* and *After-Words: Post-Holocaust Struggles with Forgiveness, Reconciliation, Justice.* Co-editor of *Encyclopedia of Holocaust Literature,* he edited and translated the English edition of *The Complete Black Book of Russian Jewry.*

Jendi Reiter is the author of *A Talent for Sadness.* Her work has won prizes from the Poetry Society of America and appeared in such publications as *Poetry, New Criterion, Mudfish,* and *Christian Century.* She is the editor of *Poetry Contest Insider,* a guide to over 650 writing contests, available at www.winningwriters.com.

Steven J. Stewart was awarded a 2005 Literature Fellowship for Translation by the National Endowment for the Arts. His book of translations of Spanish poet Rafael Pérez Estrada, *Devoured by the Moon,* was a finalist for the 2005 PEN-USA translation award. He currently lives in Rexburg, Idaho, with his wife and two children.

Steve Walker, a former editor of *Literature and Belief,* is a professor of English at Brigham Young University. His books include *Eugene England: Essays on Values in Literature* (with C. Jay Fox and Jesse S. Crisler), *Affirmations: Selections from Literature and Belief* (with C. Jay Fox), *Mourning with Those Who Mourn* (with Jane D. Brady), *Seven Ways of Looking at Susannah,* and *A Book of Mormons* (with Richard S. Van Wagoner). A specialist in the Bible as literature, he has also written articles on biblical humor, the fantastic in literature, and biblical critisicm.

Eric A. Weil teaches writing and literature at Shaw University in Raleigh, NC. His poems have appeared in *Southern Poetry Review, Poetry, American Scholar, Greensboro Review,* and other periodicals. He has also written a chapbook, *A Hourse at the Hirshhorn.*

Holly Welker is assistant professor of English and creative writing at Penn State Erie, The Behrend College. Her poetry and nonfiction have appeared in *Best American Essays 2005*, *Black Warrior Review*, *Cream City Review*, *Dialogue: A Journal of Mormon Thought*, *Gulf Coast*, *Hayden's Ferry Review*, *Iowa Review*, *PMS*, *Poetry International*, *Spoon River Poetry Review*, *Sunstone*, *TriQuarterly*, and elsewhere. Born and reared in southeastern Arizona, she currently lives and writes in northwestern Pennsylvania.